FOREWORD BY MAJOR KIM 'ROOSTER' ROSSITER, USMC (RET)

PRESIDENT, AINSLEY'S ANGELS OF AMERICA

HOLY COW

YOU WERE BORN
FOR SIGNIFICANCE

MICHAEL & SHELLY WARNER

HOLY COW

© 2022 Michael and Shelly Warner

Paperback ISBN: 978-1-66782-931-9
eBook ISBN: 978-1-66782-932-6

This book is dedicated to the first responders, medical professionals and care givers who give tirelessly of themselves for the wellbeing of others. We see you and we value you.

A person standing alone can be attacked and defeated, but two can stand back-to-back and conquer. Three are even better, for a triple-braided cord is not easily broken.
ECCLESIASTES 4:12

TABLE OF CONTENTS

FOREWORD   1

INTRODUCTION   3

PROLOGUE   5

PART ONE: ESSENCE   15

1. DOUBLE TROUBLE   17

2. SHIPWRECKS AND SEIZURES   27

3. INVESTIGATING MY OPTIONS   34

4. WHEN DESTINY MEETS DESTINATION   43

5. A LONG DARK ROAD   56

6. YOU PEOPLE NEED A REALITY CHECK   68

PART TWO: METAMORPHOSIS   85

7. THE TRANSFORMATION BEGINS   87

8. THE POWER OF LOVE   98

9. RED TEAM   107

10. NO TIME FOR TALK   114

11. THE DAY I LOST MY WHEELS   127

12. YOU GAVE ME STRENGTH   138

13. A NEW NORMAL   148

PART THREE: *BECOME*   **165**

   14. STILL ME   167

   15. TRAGEDY OR TRIUMPH   176

   16. IN TANDEM   190

   17. PASSION BECOMES PURPOSE   204

   18. WHERE THE MAGIC HAPPENS   211

   19. FAITH TO THE FINISH LINE   225

   20. IT'S NOT OVER YET   242

   ACKNOWLEDGEMENTS   253

   ABOUT THE AUTHORS   256

FOREWORD

"Hi Rooster! It's a 'GO'!! LET'S DO THIS THING!!! Let us know what we need to do next, and we are on it!" ~Team Warner

Shelly and Michael Warner sent me these words in an email on Oct 7, 2014, with an enthusiastic desire to bring our inclusive athletic program, Ainsley's Angels of America, to their community. What has followed has brought much joy and scores of opportunities for hundreds to be included across South Carolina.

Many ask, 'why me?' But my friends, Michael and Shelly, have learned to ask and teach us to ask, 'why not me?' Always seeking to help others, they believe everything happens for a reason. They also believe there are silver linings to be found, to be appreciated, to be celebrated in all situations. We have this in common. Yet, what we do not have in common, are the unique perspectives gained throughout our individual lives. By unselfishly sharing these different perspectives, Michael and Shelly bring opportunities to inspire, and to be inspired, to us all. While their humility will restrict them from saying they are an inspiration, rest assured this couple defines inspiration.

From being devastated after losing independence, to becoming a team and finding daily joy, Michael and Shelly have a way of opening our eyes to experiences that shake us to our inner core. They then make us smile as we too, realize the power these experiences can provide to form a foundation from which we can all be inspired, and then go forth to inspire others. Offering vulnerable insight into the darkness of the trials of their collective journey while outlining the 'light of opportunity,' they show us through example to "use what you have and do what you can."

Michael and Shelly have done something different from the plans they once had for themselves. They show us how our plan might have us moving along path 'A' after a long day at work, but then suddenly the reality of the master plan, that we do not have authorship of, drives us to a totally different destination. They show us life is about what we do at the new location and that our varying degrees of resilience serve as the fuel for how we will fare on arrival.

Thank you, Michael and Shelly, for the gift given to us all through this work.... the gift of understanding how to increase our resiliency in order to become better versions of ourselves, together.

Major Kim "Rooster" Rossiter, USMC (ret)

President, Ainsley's Angels of America

INTRODUCTION

Life happens. It happens to us all. We dream, plan, train for and work hard toward those goals we see for our future. We imagine what our life will be like, where we will go, the kinds of people who will surround us. It is the human way. It is the American way. But as so many of us know, only some of what we strive so hard to achieve actually happens. There is so much more we encounter in life which we did not plan for, nor did we ever want to experience given the choice. But so many of those experiences we have no control over. Things which can derail us. Our book is about not only the adversity we have been through in life but also the life we have lived despite the adversity. Life is a choice, and the choice you make determines if there's light or darkness along the way. That choice is very important, as it will determine your future.

A traumatic accident. No one would have imagined the blessings which would come from such a traumatic experience or the trajectory our life would take because of the accident. Or the drastic changes in my life which would result from a serious chronic disease I was born with. And most recently the serious health crisis my wife Shelly has gone through. Shelly and I have been on a journey together beyond anything we would have ever expected. It has been filled with tragedy, fear, loss, insecurity and challenges beyond our imagination. But more importantly, it has been a life filled with many blessings, a profound mission of purpose and a drive to make a difference in this world.

While this book is a personal story of overcoming and thriving through adversity, it is also meant to inspire. It is a love story-a glimpse into the journey of a husband-and-wife team that had the courage to not give up on each other. A team that decided by sharing the story and blessings from their own personal tragedies, they may be able to help others discover their own significance. We hope this book will push you outside of your comfort zone in how you view your own circumstances. We believe God created each one of us for significance. Our desire is to show how the power of a positive mindset can lead you to your own discovery of personal greatness.

"There is a saying in Tibetan, 'Tragedy should be utilized as a source of strength.' No matter what sort of difficulties, how painful the experience is, if we lose our hope, that is the real disaster."

—*The 14th Dalai Lama*

PROLOGUE

April 16, 2021

If you have ever dealt with someone who has seizures, you will understand what I am talking about. They are scary and leave you feeling a bit haunted. How many times in your life have you witnessed someone go through something and you wonder, *Will they make it back from this? Will they come out of this the same person, with the same personality and beautiful qualities that I love about them? Will they come out of this at all?* These are some of the questions which run through my mind as I helplessly watch Michael go through a major seizure. These are questions which start racing through my mind not only during but also after he drives away in the back of an ambulance. The terror and panic and helplessness you feel during the period you witness someone you love having a seizure can be overwhelming. You are trying to juggle exactly what it is you are seeing. *What is the first thing I need to do to help this person? Are they in a safe position? Where is my phone? Oh God, please don't leave me, please don't leave me!* You call 911: "Hello! My husband is having a seizure!" And you begin answering all the basic questions:

What is his name?

Michael

How old is he?

55

What is your name?

Shelly

Is he breathing?

I don't know! I don't know! His eyes are rolled back in his head!

Shelly… Shelly… watch his chest. Do you see it rising and falling?

Yes… yes… I think so….

Ok… every time you see it rise, I want you to say 'now,' ok?

Ok, ok…. Now… now…. Oh God, honey, stay with me, stay with me….

Shelly, Shelly… is he still breathing?

I don't know! Yes, I think so. Oh God, where are they?! Why aren't they here yet?! Michael, Michael, you are ok. You're going to be fine. You are so beautiful. Where are they?!

What is he doing now, Shelly? Is he still breathing?

Yes

Ok. Has he had any strokes or heart attacks?

No

Can you get him on his side?

What? No! He is sitting on the couch, kind of reclined with his feet up. Ok, I'll try…. Honey, honey, look at me. I can't move him; I can't move him!

What do you see? What is he doing?

He's looking off into space. His breathing isn't normal. It's erratic. I'm trying to get him on his side, but I can't do it.

Shelly… you must get him to the floor and try to get him on his side.

What?! I can't get him to the floor. His eyes are rolling back! I don't know what is happening! Where are they?!

Shelly… you must get him on the floor. Can you get him to the floor?

Ok… I'll try again. Come on, honey. Come on. Slide to the floor with me. No, Michael, don't try to stand up. It's ok. Just slide down. (I kneel on the floor and sloppily slide him to the floor, paying extra attention to his head so he doesn't fall over and hit his head on the tile. He is so stiff and fighting against me.) Ok! Ok! I got him to the floor.

Lay him down and try to get him on his side

I can't get him on his side! He won't turn that way!

Ok, Shelly. I need you to listen to me. Lay him back and ensure his chin is to the ceiling.

He is lying back, and his head is to the ceiling.

No, Shelly, I need you to ensure his chin is to the ceiling. Tilt his head back so his chin is to the ceiling. You want to keep his airway open and ensure he is not choking on his saliva or letting his tongue roll back.

Ok, ok. His chin is to the ceiling. Michael! Michael. You are ok. Where are they?! They are taking too long! Michael, I love you. You are so beautiful. You're going to be ok. They are coming to help you.

Shelly, is your dog secured in a room? Is your door unlocked so they can come into the house? When they get there, just call out to them and let them know where you are.

Yes, my dog is secured. Let me double-check to ensure I unlocked the front door. I have the lights on for them. Honey, honey! Look at me! I've got you. You're going to be ok. No! Don't stand up. Michael! Stop! He is trying to stand up! And he is fighting me. He is trying to take his shirt off. (We struggle a bit as I try to stop him and then I just give in and help him take it off.)

What is he doing now, Shelly? Is he getting violent with you?

What? No. He is just aggravated and uncomfortable. He is telling me I poisoned him. Michael, Michael... you're ok. No, honey, I didn't poison you. I hear them! I think they are finally here. Hello?! We're back here!

Are they there now, Shelly?

Yes, they're here.

Ok, I am hanging up now.

Ok. Ok. Thank you!

I go through many similar questions with the EMS crew as they come into the room and try to assess the situation and what is happening with Michael. I can concentrate on the head crew member as he asks me questions while others attend to Michael. I frantically look between the guy and Michael. More than 20 minutes has elapsed since the seizure began. Michael is starting to come out of it, calming down and starting to clear with his vision. He does not know what is going on yet, but he is starting to focus on me as I talk to him. He did not know who I was or recognize we had EMS in the house until minutes after they arrived. It takes many minutes for him to start coming around. He notices there are many people around him, but he keeps asking where they all came from. He now knows who I am but does not know what day, month or time it is. He is trying to get back on the couch and lie back with the blanket to go to sleep. He no longer has his shirt on, only his shorts and no socks. They ask him if he wants to go to the hospital and he tells them, "No, I am fine." We all agree he needs to be taken by them to get checked out at the ER. They tell me to pack a bag for him. I ask them, "Will they keep him overnight?" They don't know but say to pack it just in case. I run into our bedroom and start throwing things into a backpack. I pack a new set of underwear, new shorts, his sweatpants (it's gotten colder outside), his medicine and tooth-brush. I don't even think about his feet for shoes or socks, and I forget to throw a long-sleeved shirt for him into the bag. I race back into the room. Michael is confused and starting to look worried. He is coming around and beginning to recognize he had a seizure and is worried about me. They gently help him to the stretcher, and I tell him all will be ok, that he needs to go see the doctor. I assure him I will be following right behind them and will see him at the hospital. The group of five to six responders wheel him out the front door. I see multiple vehicles with flashing lights lighting up our street in the dark. I have no idea how many vehicles there are. I see a fire truck, a pickup with flashing lights and an ambulance. I stop looking as I don't really care how many are out there. I start running around in circles for a minute not sure what to do next. I run to the front room and let Nevo, our dog, out. He has been barking furiously this entire time and is going nuts, not sure what is happening and why all these people are at our house or who the voices are he has heard, and he's agitated with all of the commotion outside. I try to settle him with my words as I start racing in circles again trying to think. *Think, Shelly, think! What do I do next?* I go to the front door again and grab the box of dog food, which has some-how been delivered during all of this. I bring it into the house, close the front door and race to the bedroom again to change my clothes and get ready to leave for the hospital. Nevo is still barking and racing around me, following me from place to place. I talk to him the entire time I am trying to focus and settle my nerves. Should I call someone? Should I call now or wait until I get in the car? Where are the kitties? Oh… I am sure they are fine and still in the house. Hopefully they are just hiding somewhere. Where are my keys anyway? Should Nevo come with me? Maybe he should stay here at the house. But I feel like I need him with me. He can keep me company in the jeep on the drive and if I must wait in the parking lot. Will they let me in the hospital? Due to Covid? What if I can go in? Will Nevo be safe in the jeep in the parking lot? Maybe I should leave him at home. He needs to go out. Let me take him out. I must clean the cat box before I go. Oh… I must throw those items in the washing machine before I go too. I take Nevo out through the garage so I can get the jeep ready and throw the trash out on the way. I start to panic about Covid. Maybe I should not have let Michael go to the hospital. Maybe he would have been just fine at home. Did I need them to take him? Will he get Covid now that he is going into the hospital? Oh no! How will Covid affect him with seizures? What if they get worse? Should we have gotten the vaccine already? Why didn't we get the vaccine yet? What if the vaccine causes him to have an adverse reaction? Oh God, I should not have sent him to the hospital! I need to call his mom. "Nevo! Stop barking. Come here! You have to go to 'spot'!" I drag Nevo to the side of the house to do his business while I call Mike's mom at the same time. I am shaking and starting to panic. I should not have let them take him to the hospital. His mom answers and I start talking quickly, filling her in on what is happening. I am questioning my decisions and she calmly talks through the situation with me. She settles my mind by telling me I did the right thing, and he will be fine. Nevo is barking again and running circles around me with the leash while he is kicking up the grass. I start to unravel and feel tears coming on. Susan is still calm, gently talking me through what I need to do and telling me to leave Nevo at home. Oh no, here comes the neighbor calling to me. "I have to go; the neighbor is coming. I'll call you later," I tell Susan. "Just a minute, Catherine," I shout out as I move to run Nevo back in the house. I settle him down, give him his treat and tell him to 'protect house.' I grab my stuff and race back out to the garage. Catherine is walking into the garage now and I quickly share with her what is happening. She is so sweet and is very concerned for both Michael and me. She is in her pj's with flip-flops on. I literally laugh for a minute as I feel sorry for scaring her but am touched at her concern and that she came outside as she has. She offers to take Nevo. I share with her he should be fine and that I will stay in touch to let her know what happens with Michael. She offers to drive me to the hospital, but I assure her I will be fine. She will be my communication link to the other neighbors. I am very grateful for her as she leaves to go back home, and I jump in the jeep to leave for the hospital.

People tell me I am strong. That I am good at handling situations like Michael's seizures. Susan assures me I make the right decisions for us both and she is fully comfortable knowing her precious son is in my care. After all the dust settles and we realize Michael is going to be ok, we go through the processes at the hospital until he can be released hours later. I have him wait in the vestibule while I go get the jeep because it is cold outside, and he only has on a short-sleeve shirt. He has gotten cold air into his lungs, and he can't stop coughing. When we get home, he goes into the house, and I take Nevo out once again. He is nuts! He is barking like crazy, running back and forth between us and trying to make it outside at the same time. He has all of those pent-up nerves and energy and once again has to go to the bathroom. He does not stop barking even after we go back in the house, and he races to find his daddy. He is barking, whining and crying, all at the same time. He is so distraught at what has transpired and that he was unable to protect us and take care of his daddy through it all. We work to settle him down. Michael calls his mom as it nears 11:00 p.m. I walk around the house doing small chores to resettle for the night. We have not eaten yet but neither of us is very hungry. I know Michael needs to eat something and he will not eat if I don't eat something. So, I reheat a couple of the steamed potatoes I had made earlier in the day, and we each eat one before we head to bed. We cry ourselves to sleep as we hold hands and say our prayers, sharing how grateful we are for each other and for God. It is almost 1:00 a.m. now. I wake back up at 4:40 a.m. and Michael is on the very edge of the bed, turned away from me. I put my hand under his shirt, on his back, to ensure he is breathing. I can feel his breathing through his back, but I struggle to determine if it is normal. Is he breathing regularly? I lie there for a bit, not wanting Nevo to get up again, but I can't resist checking on Michael more closely. And I must pee. So, I get up and gently flash the light from my phone near his face. Are his eyes open? Are they open because I have woken him up or are they staying open as if in a seizure? I study him a moment before he starts to speak. Whew! He is ok. I tell him I must go to the bathroom and will be right out. I come out a moment later, and now Nevo plus our two kitties are up and circling because they think it is time for breakfast. Damn it! Nevo needs to go out again. I quickly dress and head to the kitchen to take him out. I will feed all the fur babies when I get back inside. As I am standing out in the tree area behind our house, in the dark with the flashlight searching for snakes before we take another step, I wait for Nevo to do his thing. My mind and my heart are still racing with nerves and worry. My stomach still hurts, and I feel like I am going to vomit. I think about our scenario from the night before and I am weary from it. How many people go through this experience of a life-and-death moment multiple times in their lives? How many have had to watch loved ones suffer and feel so helpless when you can't help them? When you can't keep them from the struggle? How many continuously replay these moments in their minds and live in a state of worry and concern, always watchful for the next moment of a seizure? Always in a state of awareness of behavioral patterns and responses from one you love in an effort to determine if they are having another seizure or not? What the hell causes these things? What more can we do to try to prevent them? We do everything we can possibly think of to try to live as healthily as possible to protect our health and hopefully prevent more seizures. But they still come. Sometimes I feel like I have PTSD or something. No wonder I often feel like I am in a freeze-frame scenario. Like I am waiting for the next thing to happen. I often feel like crying for no reason. I am glad I am strong, but sometimes I don't want to be the strong one. I don't feel like I can hold up that responsibility all the time. The weight of it is so heavy. The fear of *what if I am not strong? What if I can't do this or I make the wrong decision? What if something happens to me? Who will take care of Michael? Who will take care of our babies and all the other stuff?* I know this is something too many of us go through on a regular basis. I guess it is just part of life. We have often talked about missing out on not having kids. But when situations like a major seizure happen, I recognize my own limitations and know it is just one of the reasons why this was not to be part of our lives. I am grateful for God knowing what is best for us when we have not known it for ourselves.

I pray He continues to guide us both with His love and to share insight and wisdom with me, especially in those critical moments when I need it most. I don't know how people make it through the tough times in life if they do not believe in God. I can't imagine the difficulty and loneliness of not having God to walk through life with you, especially in the midst of the most challenging moments. I am grateful for Him. Thank goodness for this as He has carried us through many unexpected trials in our life already.

PART ONE

ESSENCE

ONE

DOUBLE TROUBLE

You made all the delicate, inner parts of my body and knit
me together in my mother's womb. Thank you for making
me so wonderfully complex! Your workmanship is mar-
velous-how well I know it!

Psalms 139: 13-14

June 1965

My fight began before I even entered this world. Seven weeks early
from her due date, sitting in her kitchen talking to my uncle, my mom's
water broke. It was June 23, 1965, in Detroit, Michigan. It was time my
twin brother and I decided to make our way into this world. For hours the
two of us fought it out to see who would enter the world first. Bob won that
first battle and entered the world on June 24, 1965, and I followed behind
him three minutes later. The unexpected timing of our entrance would

not be the first surprise or challenge of the day. The next surprise? There were two of us! Yes, you read that correctly. In 1965, in Detroit, Michigan, ultrasounds were not yet available to prepare them for this news. Can you imagine what a shock this must have been? I was born into a family with two older sisters, Mary, 3, and Kathleen, 2, just babies themselves, and now a twin brother older by three minutes. I instantly became the baby of the family. Being that they did not even realize they were having twins, I would later wonder, *Was I even a baby they wanted?* But I have always believed God saves the best for last, so I guess this takes care of that thought! The first big obstacle for me and my brother was to make it out of the hospital in good health. We discovered that would not be easy. But it would turn out that we were two tough little boys with a determination to take on the world. From the onset, our parents believed we were fighters, and their optimism would be severely tested through our first 48 hours in intensive care.

Bob weighed 3 lb., 8 oz, and I was a breech baby weighing in at 3 lb., 4 oz. I like to imagine this moment as me kicking him out of the womb and out of my way so I could come into this world and get the party started. God planted the belief in me from inception that I was born for significance. We were both immediately taken and placed into incubators for critical care. Our lungs were not yet fully formed, and we were struggling to survive on our own. We would miss the snuggling and cuddling of Mom and Dad in these first days, as we were each placed into our own little protected world. Our health was so fragile, our parents could initially see us only through a glass wall looking into the nursery. The enormity of the situation was overwhelming to my young parents. Here they were, a young couple early in their marriage and already with two young daughters at home. Now they were in a scenario with the shock of a premature birth and the fact that there were two babies. Twins! And both of their beautiful boys were in a fight for their lives. The level of emotion, the joy, fear, anxiety, worry, love and so much more were swirling through them both as they looked through that glass wall into our plexiglass domes. They could not even hold us and give us the comfort, care and love we so desperately needed. The first touch our premature little bodies would receive would be from those precious neonatal nurses caring for us. Sticking their arms through the round holes on the sides of our new safe haven, they worked hard to calm us through our cries and provide the care we needed. Overwhelmed, confused and a bit fearful, my parents had to rely on the wonderful care of those nurses and doctors who watched over us for those first critical 48 hours. My mom talks about those first days with gratitude for the two key pediatricians attending to us, especially the one who would check in every day, whether he was on duty or not. He was a beacon of strength and comfort for my mom during that uncertain time. With two other young toddlers to care for, it was necessary for my mom to return home after about three days in the hospital. It was challenging to say the least to try and juggle time and energy with my sisters at home and knowing Bob and I were fighting for life in the hospital. What made it worse was we only had one car for the family and my dad needed it for work. Because of that, she could not visit us every day. Thank goodness we had angels on our medical team providing us the care we needed in those initial weeks. Bob and I soon gained strength and graduated from the incubators to isolettes. No longer enclosed in plexiglass, we were both still protected in this new world with the extra warmth and protection of our new cribs. Although we were tiny entering this world, we actually lost weight in our struggle to survive. Bob dropped down to 2 lb., 10 oz, and I dropped down to 2 lb., 8 oz. We were only 18 inches long. This posed a bit of a problem for us, as we needed to hit a goal weight of 5 lb. before we would be allowed to go home. We called the hospital home for the first two months of our lives. In a way, we see this as a blessing, as it gave my mom and dad some time to come to terms with the realization that they were bringing two babies home from the hospital, not just one. It provided time to absorb and accept this truth and establish what additional plans would be necessary to finally bring us home. Bob reached his goal weight of 5 lb. first and was able to go home ten days before I did. I guess I wanted to hang out with all those pretty nurses a while longer and bask in all the extra attention I could get from them without him stealing the show. As twins, we would find ourselves competing for attention throughout our lives in many different ways.

Once we were able to go home finally, we became part of a larger family unit. With my dad working full time at Ford Motor Company, my mom had her hands full with four babies, all under the age of four at one time. Her full-time job was a 24-7 responsibility, struggling to keep her sanity while trying to care for us all and maintain the household. My sisters already were a lot to handle. They loved their new little 'toys' though. Two new squirmy dolls for them to play with and help care for. My mom says she often felt like a juggler, always having one or more balls in the air with each of us vying for her full attention at once. I can't really imagine how difficult it was, but it gives me comfort knowing that I was the saving grace as the 'good kid.' Although my mom wore a cape and had many superpowers, she still came to the realization she could not do it all herself as much as she tried. Fortunately, my parents were able to hire some help for the first year. They found a young woman, who came in once a week to help clean and do other chores relating to having so many little ones to care for. She was a lifesaver in that she gave my mom an hour or two of time for herself. This allowed her to be able to share a cup of coffee with a neighbor, who had a son around the same age as me and my brother. Today, this would be considered a mental health break. It was a welcome respite from my mom's hectic life. The other incredibly important addition to the family was the splurge of a new portable dishwasher. This helped to dry up a few of the tears of frustration my mom surely shed with all the work she had to do. I can only imagine what a handful my brother, sisters and I must have been for her. It took nine months before my mom and dad had their first night out alone together. No one was willing to watch all four of us at once, which was revealing. It took two different people to allow them to get some time alone. My grandmother took my sisters overnight and a daring friend of my mom's took me and my brother for the evening. This simple act of kindness gave my parents a necessary break just to enjoy each other for the simple act of a dinner out.

As we grew, I progressed more slowly than my brother. The trauma I went through at birth resulted in my facing multiple challenges in my life. These challenges started early and began showcasing themselves in my delay regarding learning skills such as sitting up, crawling and walking. Also showcasing itself early was my character trait of being a fighter and being willing to do the hard work to get where I needed to go. By the age of 18 months, I had caught up to my brother and we were on the same developmental track. We were two happy, healthy, rambunctious boys. Although we were identical twins, our parents didn't have any trouble telling us apart. My mom said we had sweet and endearing personalities but both unique in our own ways. She said we had different temperaments from the first day, and she believed this was an effect of nature rather than nurture. God's creative design. I also had a special little smile and a cute way of tilting my head when I looked at her. Although the tilt of my head was a slight concern for my mom from the very beginning, my family considered this to be a personality quirk.

When I was around three, my parents began to notice I would tilt my head more often when looking at them, and it had seemed to become more obvious in comparison to the photos taken since birth. This also explains the infamous picture of me and my 'Lurch' smile, which had become a family favorite. To me though, this was a terrible photo of me with that head tilt and a goofy smile. Now when I look at it, it makes me grateful, and I thank God I don't smile that way anymore. My parents decided to investigate this odd quirk with our pediatrician to determine if there was something more going on with me. It was time for a vision test. The pediatrician who tested my vision happened to be the same one who had spent 30 hours with me during those critical first days after my birth. He knew me very well. Within a few months of that vision test, it was determined that I had amblyopia or 'lazy eye.' Two symptoms of this condition are head tilting and eyes that appear to not work together. There are several causes associated with the increased risk of lazy eye, including premature birth and a small size at birth. Well, that definitely included me. Best treatment results for amblyopia are achieved when it is treated before the age of 7. I was 3.5 years old when it was decided I would go through treatment to correct the problem. This was the beginning of so many steps to come to assist me through the trials I would endure throughout my life. But even at a young age, my parents said I took it all in stride. Eye patches and corrective eyewear were accepted treatments for amblyopia, so my parents decided we would do both. It's funny to think of today that my brother and I were forming our identities at this critical young age, yet as identical twins, we couldn't have been farther apart. Me, with the smaller tilting head, Lurch smile and now an eye patch and glasses, making me look like a pirate or some crazy comic book character. And my brother was just a good-looking, happy little boy. Something which makes me feel a bit better about my own oddities is to look back at family pictures and see how my mom dressed my sisters. We were one crazy-looking family, and I fit right in. I'm assuming that in a strange way, I felt that the eye patch made me look cool. But apparently my mom said I didn't like the glasses. It took two years and many frustrating moments for my parents, but we ultimately achieved optimum results with my vision reaching near 20/20.

My challenges continued into third grade. It was at this time I started to struggle with schoolwork. Diagnosed with a learning disability, I began to receive extra help to accomplish some of the basics. My parents hired a tutor for a short time, but I apparently didn't appreciate this, so I continued to struggle through the years on my own. While I was still dealing with a learning disability, verbally I did excellent work. My challenge was with writing, spelling and connectivity of words. Despite these challenges, I just continued along with a drive to achieve at my own pace. In sixth grade, a suggestion was made by the school for me to seek counseling. This was a suggestion to help ease the transition into junior high school and to strengthen my reading skills. We found through counseling that part of my issue was in my struggle of finding my own identity and self image as an identical twin. My brother and I were discovering our own space, as our parents encouraged us to find our own individuality. It wasn't easy developing a socially acceptable self image as 'Lurch, the Pirate' while my twin brother had seemingly no issues. But we were both determined to have our own unique identities.

Although others thought it was cute to dress us alike, my parents did not agree and therefore stopped doing this at a very young age. They also encouraged us to foster our own individual choices in sports. Playing sports was not only a healthy outlet for energy and development but also a good exercise in hand–eye coordination. As young boys, we played just about every sport you can think of. Having the ability to choose the sport which best fit our own interests was a turning point in developing our own identities. As a family, we didn't have the money for fancy hockey equipment, so playing hockey was not an option. Playing for our beloved Red Wings? Well, that would just be one of those sports fantasies that would remain just a dream. My dad was the neighborhood baseball coach, so baseball became our first sport of choice. Bob and I played on my dad's team, where it was discovered Bob had a natural talent for baseball. He had good hand–eye coordination, was quick on his feet and had a great work ethic on the field. Me on the other hand? Not so much. I soon discovered this was not my sport. I did make an effort even though dragging myself to the baseball field to play right field and first base was almost as exciting as working with that tutor they had once tried. I was a kid who was looking for more excitement than baseball had to offer, and I wasn't a big fan of all the rules and slow pace of the game. I wanted to keep moving. Standing and waiting for a ball to be hit to me out in right field was as exciting to me as watching paint dry. It was agonizing to be at the baseball field just waiting for something to happen. It turned out that the only part of baseball I was good at was getting hit by a pitch. I guess that was a result of my poor hand–eye coordination. Babe Ruth once said, "Every strike brings me closer to the next home run." I, on the other hand, felt every strike and 'hit by pitch' (HBP) pushed me farther away from the game. I'm sure my dad wasn't thrilled every time I walked to the plate, but I must admit it was fun being the coach's son. I found I loved being outside in the fresh air. A natural transition for me was shifting to the game of soccer. Soccer was a sport of endless energy that tested and challenged my endurance capabilities while at the same time helped me with my struggling hand–eye coordination. It was a perfect fit for me and did not compromise the family budget. Instead of having the need for expensive hockey equipment, my mom used two old TV guides and placed them in my socks to use as shin guards. With a T-shirt and shorts, I was ready to play. We lived in Livonia, a suburb of Detroit, which was known for having a great youth soccer program. Bob decided to try soccer as well. We played on many teams through the YMCA and often played the same position. We were both forwards, primarily wingers on the opposite sides of the field. I was known for having a strong left foot and often played left wing, and Bob was a right winger. Who would have known then that the discipline and physical conditioning from the game of soccer would play an important part of my recovery later in life?

As we grew older, Bob decided to focus on his favorite sport of baseball while I pursued my passion in soccer. As twins, we were close as brothers, but we had the same struggles and experiences most siblings have going through their teenage years and high school. We loved each other but we had our own sets of friends and competed as all boys do for the attention of the girls. It was a toss-up of who had the cooler car and the better sense of dress and style and who was better looking and more popular in school. We both worked during high school but there too, we pursued different directions. My first work experience was what any high school kid with a big appetite desired—working in a fast-food restaurant. My top choice? Taco Bell. That was a fun experience with the added benefit of receiving free food while working. That was until I was tired of smelling like burritos and sweating into the beans. It was then that I decided to upgrade and go to work at Burger King. I had a fabulous one-day experience there. I went to orientation, received my uniform and went home with my new schedule for work. It took only one moment of trying on that uniform and hat before Bob laughed his way out of the house. I took off that uniform, folded it back up and returned it with my apologies while declining the job offer. My next new employment adventure was into the world of retail. I began working in loss prevention at Meijer (a national grocery chain) before moving on to Marshalls Department Stores. Unknowingly, these would be my first steps into a career path I didn't even know would be my future. While I began down my own path into the world of the service industry, Bob began his journey into the world of construction, working for a company owned and operated by good friends of ours. Although it was backbreaking work for Bob, it paid better than my world of restaurants and retail. We were each finding our own way and forging our own paths for the future.

TWO

SHIPWRECKS AND SEIZURES

Blessed is the one who perseveres under trial because,
having stood the test, that person will receive the crown of
life that the Lord has promised to those who love him.

— *James 1:12*

Have you experienced something in your life which changed the trajectory of your future? Maybe it was something very difficult which you felt detoured you away from the path you wanted to go down. Did that detour bring about a change in your life you would have never chosen for yourself but one which ended up bringing something very positive if unexpected? Out of the darkness came light? This has been part of my story on more than one occasion. High school ended on a high note of celebration and victory. It was 1983 and we believed the world was at our fingertips. I had been part of Michigan's first high school 'Class A' State Championship soccer team. What a rush! We finished the season with a 22–0 record. At that time, no other team in the history of Michigan soccer had achieved this kind of record, and I am not sure if one has done it since. We were unbeatable. It was a feeling of power and euphoria. I would come to tap into those feelings many times in the coming years of my life. But now it was time to make the transition into college and take my passion and talent for soccer with me. After graduation, a good friend and soccer buddy, Dan Laurie, asked me to join him on a family boat trip. Dan had a family of experienced boaters, and they belonged to a Sea Ray boat club. The plan was to accompany Dan's family, along with multiple other families from the boat club, on a two-week adventure. The trip would take us through the Great Lakes from Detroit into Canada. This was going to be a trip of a lifetime, stopping in strategic ports along the way and exploring the beautiful scenic waters of our Canadian neighbors. This meant spending quality time with Dan and his family, feasting on great food, having fun in the water, getting tons of sun and snorkeling into shipwrecks along the way. This trip of a lifetime would set the course for the rest of my life.

The thought of experiencing the beautiful waters of Ontario was exciting, even though it started out a little rough. From the moment we set off from the marina I started to feel a bit queasy and found myself a little uneasy. I wasn't a regular fan of being out on the water, but I sure wasn't going to pass up this trip. Shortly into the voyage, the water became rough, and I found myself hanging off the back of the boat hurling my lunch. Feeling embarrassed as the guest who couldn't handle the waves, I relaxed after Dr. Laurie, Dan's father, assured us he had never seen waves that high. Although this did make me feel a bit better, I was already looking forward to getting my feet back on dry land. Soon we would be making a stop at the first of many marinas we would visit in the coming two weeks. These stops would be loads of fun and would include meeting many new and interesting people. Our group of boats would dock together, and we would spend the day swimming, snorkeling, playing some soccer and simply hanging out together. I have great memories of music blaring our favorite rock 'n' roll from the deck of the boat, enjoying the people and the great outdoors and drinking our favorite beverages. The days would usually end with our large group going to dinner at a local hot spot and sharing stories from our adventures. One of our stops was in Georgian Bay, Ontario. After an incredible day of fun on the water, we went to dinner at a local seafood restaurant near the marina. Our huge party was cheerful and boisterous as we enjoyed conversation and our dinners. I was having the time of my life. The next thing I remember was coming to and looking around as I slowly regained consciousness. Sitting in a chair, I looked down at a long table which seated the families from our trip. I couldn't understand why everyone was staring at me. Within minutes, Dr. Laurie and other unknown people were asking me if I was ok. I couldn't answer that question because I had no idea what had just happened. I was very uncomfortable and embarrassed with this unwanted attention. Unfortunately, this would be a feeling I would experience many times in the years to come. I felt rigid, almost stone-like, and had a terrible headache. Because of my lack of recollection leading to this moment, this part of the story is best explained by my mom, who had received a late-night phone call:

"The call came in as I was on another call. The operator interrupted and asked if I would take a call from Dr. Laurie in Georgian Bay, Canada. In the pre-cell phone era, a call could be interrupted by an operator in an emergency. Dr. Laurie was a medical professional, a dentist, so he was well

versed in medical issues. He explained to me what had happened and that he thought Michael had suffered a grand mal seizure as a result of sunstroke. He felt that Michael was fine for now and it would be ok for him to finish the trip. We were prepared to travel to get him at this point, but Dr. Laurie reassured us Michael would be watched over and well taken care of. He did advise me that I should plan for a complete workup for Michael with our doctor when they returned. I was very concerned at this point but trusted his advice and we allowed Michael to continue on with the trip."

Once we returned from the trip, I discovered my mom had already made plans for me to see some specialists. A work acquaintance of my dad's had a very important connection for us. This connection was the chief of staff at Northwest Grace Hospital in Detroit. He had made arrangements for me to see a neurosurgeon and they were ready for me to be admitted upon my arrival home. To be able to have made an appointment so quickly had been an extreme favor and blessing offered to my parents. I understand why my mom always said, "It pays to know people."

So, it began upon my being admitted to Grace Hospital. Immediately they started CT scans, an MRI, blood tests and more. I was transported to Harper Hospital, Downtown Detroit, for an angiogram and then back to Grace. The angiogram was an invasive and delicate test which went from the groin to the brain by inserting a dye to find any abnormalities. Ultimately, they concluded that there was an area of the lower right hemisphere of my brain which was abnormal. They did not know if it was a tumor or a congenital abnormality that I was born with and believed it had never been active until now. Was this another result of being the unlucky twin or possibly the result of actively using my head clearing the ball in soccer? We did not really know, but the doctors quickly dismissed the soccer idea. It certainly was coincidental that I had just finished an aggressive and long year of soccer and as a defenseman, my head was my weapon of choice to clear the ball. Although we pursued this possibility, the doctors claimed there was not enough research to connect this type of ongoing head trauma with seizures. We challenge that assumption to this day, although this theory has never been proven for me. Despite not having a full understanding of the origin of the abnormality in my brain, my medical team felt it was caused at birth. They decided it was too deep-seated and too risky to pursue surgical intervention. Whether it was the sun, the excitement, having motion sickness on the boat or something else, it really could not be determined what had triggered my grand mal seizure. But the tonic clonic seizure from that boat trip was the first of its kind I was known to have had and I was diagnosed with epilepsy. I would soon discover this type of seizure behavior would not be a normal or regular occurrence for me. The typical seizure behavior I would experience throughout my life going forward was different from that of a grand mal seizure. My specific seizure disorder diagnosis is a complex partial seizure. This type of seizure is characterized by a partial loss of cognitive function for a brief period. I have little to no advance warning of one coming on, and afterward, I can return to my normal activity as usual. Often, my seizures are so subtle, others do not even realize I am having one. This would come into play as both an advantage for me and a detriment in my future.

Epilepsy can be explained as a combination of abnormal brain activity resulting from a wide variety of triggers. My mom had a difficult time accepting this and was hoping that there was medication or treatment for it. Both of my parents sincerely wished they could have traded places with me, but their strong and healthy son would have to face this diagnosis forever. After a recovery period from the initial tests and procedures, our family took a well-deserved vacation to our cottage in upper Michigan. Some rest and relaxation for everyone was exactly what we all needed. Following that trip, there would be additional CT scans, visits to the neurologist and working to find the right combination of medications to keep any future seizures under control. Unfortunately, this all was taking place as I was preparing and getting ready for college soccer. I had received a partial scholarship to play, but my playing soccer that first year of college would no longer be possible. Even though the doctors said soccer did not cause my epilepsy, they didn't want me to take any chances, at least for a while. So, I was forced to make an important decision. A decision later described by my parents as courageous and one which proved to be an example of the person I am. I talked with the coaches and agreed to stay on with the team, to be included in the workouts but not participate in games. Essentially, I became the team manager for the first part of the season and quickly learned how to wrap ankles. This taught me so much about myself and helped me to appreciate the game on an entirely different level. From the sidelines, I became a student of the discipline and work ethic it took each player to play the game successfully. Witnessing the game and other players in this way gave me a competitive edge others did not have. When I finally made it back onto the field, I felt confident and prepared. I had a better understanding of my position and a clear picture of how each player and position works together to accomplish a goal. This was a critical life lesson to learn for both on the field and off. It was also a key moment for me to take an obstacle and turn it into triumph.

Being diagnosed with epilepsy shed new light on other small incidents I had experienced growing up, which had been dismissed at the time as strange and unexplained behavior. For example, I had a small fender bender one day as I was approaching stopped traffic at a light. I was slowing down but I did not stop, and I bumped the car in front of me. Fortunately, no one was hurt and there was no real damage to the cars. I had another situation where I veered off the road and hit a fire hydrant one snowy evening. Not only did I hit the fire hydrant, but my car also continued on into the yard, dragging the fire hydrant with it. Before anyone showed up to help with the accident, I backed my car up and drove home, which was only a few houses away. I walked into the house and told my mom, "I hit something." Of course the fire department responded due to the volcano of water erupting from the damaged fire hydrant. When the police showed up, I told them I had seen headlights from another car coming straight for me and I had been trying to avoid hitting that car. At the time, we considered my strange behavior with this accident to be attributed to the slick streets from the snow, an effort to avoid an accident with another car and my being overtired from work. We would later come to think of those incidents as having possibly been different forms of seizures. But at the time, this connection had not yet been made. These were incidents I had prior to that infamous boat trip and diagnosis. I went for years after that epilepsy diagnosis without incident. Maybe I just did a good job of hiding my seizures from others and even from myself. But this diagnosis would become a very critical component in my future. Not only would it be critical for my health, but it would also factor into many other aspects of my life, especially my professional world. Interestingly, it would also turn out to be one of the many blessings molding me into the person I would become.

THREE

INVESTIGATING MY OPTIONS

Keep on asking and you will receive what you ask for.
Keep on seeking and you will find. Keep on knocking and
the door will be opened to you.

—Matthew 7:7

My first year out of high school I had decided to attend the local community college. Because of the scholarship I received, I believed it was a perfect environment for me to begin taking the core classes for my college curriculum. I felt as if I were moving beyond my seizure diagnosis and reclaiming the life I believed I should be living. I had shifted from being the team manager and was now, once again, an active member of the soccer team and in the best shape of my life. Soccer consumed five days a week including practices and games. At the same time, I was a criminal justice student taking 12–18 credit hours/week to meet the requirements for my scholarship. This fell in line with my ultimate professional goal of becoming a Michigan State Trooper. All of this was being accomplished while working full-time as a store detective at Meijer.

As an undercover store detective, I spent my hours in the store investigating internal and external dishonesty. I was a professional people watcher and catching shoplifters and protecting the store were my specialties. I quickly discovered I had a good investigative eye and loved the adrenaline rush of apprehending shoplifters. I could not deny the way my position filled my day with anticipation and fed the thrill of the hunt to catch the bad guys. Not only did I work for Meijer, but I was also recruited and then went on to work at Marshalls Department Stores in a multi-location capacity. This was a promotion and new challenge for me, which came with a higher income. Enjoying my time with Marshalls and feeling challenged in my position, I settled into a comfortable routine of work, school and soccer. Until that is the buzz of excitement, for a new, well-known retailer coming to the Detroit area caught my attention. Target Stores was coming to Michigan and was about to open the first of its stores in the state in the Metro Detroit area. Target had a reputation for being the 'Best of the Best' for loss prevention, utilizing state-of-the art technology as well as being known for top hiring standards of good, professional people to protect their stores. How could I not be part of this new company expansion into my state and hometown area? So, I did not waste time and went to fill out an application in the hopes of becoming a part of their team. Four hours later and after an extensive psychological examination was completed, I found myself going home and waiting to hear back from them. The 600-question examination was a bit of a surprise and was something I had never experienced before, despite my previous retail experience. I was amazed at the scrupulous hiring practices and yet impressed with their high standards. The security leadership team for Target was experienced and intentional on whom they were looking for to fill their positions. Fortunately, they saw potential in me and decided they wanted me to become part of their team. A job offer was extended, and I gratefully accepted. This company was driven for success and to be an industry leader. Target seemed to be a perfect fit for me, and I was fired up and ready to start.

Target was a great match for me professionally, and I quickly made my way up the ranks from a store protection specialist and security officer to one of only two senior security officers in the entire Metro Detroit area. It was an honor to be selected for this position and one which I took with full attention and seriousness. But don't misunderstand me—my priority of becoming a police officer was still my top goal. Soccer and schoolwork continued as top priorities as well. My struggles due to my learning disabilities continued to challenge me daily. I worked very hard to maintain average grades while my friends seemed to move through their classes with ease. Good grades did not always come easily, and I never took one for granted. I had to focus and be disciplined with my time to ensure I stayed on top of my grades. One day after class, a professor invited me and my friend Ken back to his office at the state police post. He was a distinguished member of the State Police Department, and he had our full respect. Knowing we both were intent on pursuing higher education in law enforcement, he wanted to discuss our plans and options for the future. He was enthusiastic and supportive of our career focus and wanted to share some advice regarding our next steps. When we entered his office, he stood up, asking us to follow him. We followed him into the basement of the post where the training room was located. I must admit it was an honor to be in his presence and to have this kind of attention. I'm not sure what Ken and I did to deserve this special treatment, but we soon realized there was much more to come. While we sat at a training table, our distinguished instructor unlocked a huge cabinet and opened the double doors. He selected two training packets from every shelf and then made two separate piles of these materials on the table in front of us. The stacks seemed to tower over us as we sat there wondering what was happening. Softly he said, "If you are going to take your education to a four-year university, you are going to need to be prepared." We were amazed he had taken the time and attention to focus on each of us. We thanked him and walked out of the post with our hands full. It was time to get busy! We had a lot of studying to do. We would soon find out how important these materials would be to our future, and Ken and I both planned to use these resources to the best of our ability.

I was planning on attending Ferris State University upon completing my first year at the community college. Ferris State was recognized as one of the top criminal justice schools in the state. The campus was located about three hours north of Livonia, where I still lived with my family. I was excited for the opportunity and could not wait for this adventure which would take me away from home and bring me a few steps closer to my desire in becoming a police officer. Having two trucks loaded and ready with our limited belongings, Ken and I waved to our families and hit the road. Although I was riding high on adrenaline and excitement, I was still a bit apprehensive. After all, I wasn't the best student, and this was my first experience living away from home. But just as I did throughout the rest of my life, I was willing to go after it with everything I had. As much as I loved the game of soccer and it had played an integral role in my life to this point, my focus at Ferris would be on my studies. It was time to put the soccer ball on the shelf.

The criminal justice curriculum was broken down into three sections, all of which covered the career options one could expect to have in the field. These options included the specialist track (those wanting to go into law enforcement as police officers or investigators), security administration (careers in the private sector) and probation (corrections, parole and probation). My focus was set on the specialist track. Becoming a police officer was what I wanted to do in my career. Even though I was an experienced loss-prevention officer, I had always felt that my security experience was training me for something greater down the road. I wanted to make a difference and help people on another level. At the time, I believed being a police officer was the best way for me to make this impact.

Being an average student, I quickly realized that I had to work a little harder just to get by. It didn't help my self-esteem watching each of my roommates effortlessly excel in their classes. But each one of them helped me along the way to get through those dreaded math and science classes. One afternoon, during one of my core criminal justice classes, the dean of Criminal Justice walked in to make an announcement to the class. He announced the university was opening a new campus bookstore and after months of construction, they were ready to hire qualified people to work as security officers. Really? Was there truly a need for an undercover security team to protect books from theft? I had been driving back to the Detroit area every two or three weekends to maintain my position as a senior security officer with Target, so I hadn't been interested in picking up another job on campus working security. But after the announcement was made, I thought this might be right up my alley. It sure would not hurt to fill out an application and learn more about the bookstore. So, after class I headed over to the student center to check things out. When I walked in, the main hallway was loaded with students sitting along both walls filling out applications. Even with my vast experience I was a bit intimidated. I was not a great student, and I felt like this would be a factor in how I would be critically assessed for the position. I turned in my application and went to return to my seat. Before I even made it there, I heard, "Michael Warner?" I turned around and the person waved me back to the front of the line. I walked through the door and was politely asked to step into an office where a group of administrators sat among piles of applications. A gentleman spoke up and commented on my experience. After fielding multiple basic questions from this group, they ended our meeting with one final question: "When can you start"?

From $5 architectural pencils to $120 chemistry books, some of the cases I resolved working for the bookstore were a first for me. It was an eye-opener but not surprising that even students took advantage of the five-finger discount. The new bookstore itself was a beautiful building. Everything was new and with high-end fixtures and impactful signing. It reminded me of Hudson's, one of our favorite department stores we shopped growing up. It was fresh, upscale and modern. After establishing myself as an effective loss-prevention specialist protecting profits, I found myself being recruited to also work at a campus grocery store. I agreed to work some extra shifts and quickly found myself freezing in the milk cooler as I sat on milk crates monitoring the shelves of liquor. In Michigan, liquor, beer and wine are sold in grocery stores and readily available on shelves. This can be too easy of a target item to resist for many shoplifters, students included. Just when I thought I had seen it all through my years of experience, I encountered a new situation. In front of me, in the aisle, stood a large, 6'5" guy with cheese, steaks and bourbon. As he quickly concealed some of each of these items into his sweatpants, I knew I would soon be flashing my badge to him out on the sidewalk. Come to find out, this guy was a senior football player and lived in my dorm. Well, that was awkward. Years later, as my twin brother was working out at a Vic Tanny fitness center in the Detroit area, he was approached by an intimidating guy. Bob noticed two guys watching him closely while he was working out and could not figure out what their problem was. Finally, one of the guys approached Bob and asked if he had gone to school at Ferris State. Feeling a bit uncomfortable, Bob was nervous to answer this question. He did attend for a semester, so he told them yes. The man pointed over to the 6'5" monster busting out of his shirt lifting weights and said, "My friend over there thought you were the guy who caught him shoplifting. He said you treated him well and just wanted to say 'hello' and 'thank you' for your respect during that situation." This was obviously a case of mistaken identity, but Bob was certainly relieved the scenario had ended on a positive note. It was a great compliment for him to hear this about his twin brother. What an interesting example of how much fun it can be to have an identical twin. The learning lesson here? Never underestimate whom you are interacting with and how that interaction may come back to you somehow in the future. Keep it positive!

Continuing with my focus on my studies and work, I felt confident my practical experience would be beneficial as I transitioned into being a police officer. I believed things were going well and right on track for me to transition into the career I had been diligently working so hard toward. That is, until one day at the end of one of my senior classes, the professor asked me and three other students to stay after class. This time it was not about my security experience or a fun, new opportunity. I was flagged as a concern because of my medical history. My seizure disorder and diagnosis had caught up with me. I had always believed if I stayed healthy and fit, followed the direction of my neurologist and was diligent with my medication, that I could keep my seizures under control. I had believed this would be sufficient for me to accomplish my goals of becoming a police officer. Unfortunately, this was not to be my reality. It was explained to me that it had been determined I was not qualified to be a police officer due to health concerns. My medical team would not sign off on the proper authorization to ensure my safety because my seizures could not be controlled 100%. It was deemed to be unsafe for me and others if I were to assume a position as an officer, carrying a weapon and being involved in high-stress, unpredictable situations. The possibilities were too great of something terrible happening if I had a seizure amid a bad situation. It was shocking for me to hear this and to try and absorb what this news meant for me and my future. For the first time in my life, seizures would stand in the way of me achieving a goal I had set for myself. What was I to do now? I remember walking across campus, back to my dorm in shock, disbelief and embarrassment. Being told I did not measure up was not something I wanted to hear nor was I willing to accept. Thankfully, the structure of the program I was in and the way the curriculum was designed allowed me to easily transfer my credit hours from the specialist track to the security administrative track. I would not lose any credit hours. Whew! Even better? The practical experience I had accumulated throughout the years in my loss-prevention positions set me up for greater opportunities than I even knew existed with the retailer I was already working for-Target Stores. This was not the path I had envisioned for myself and my life, but God obviously knew better and had bigger plans for me.

With my college days behind me, I was now fully engaged with what I loved to do. Protecting people and stores and working with good people. I had enough experience and great results to set me on a firm path to climb the corporate ladder. I knew I was good, and I was going to be even better. My mission was to be the best at what I did, and I had that passion driving me. One added benefit of pursuing this career path in the private sector in comparison to being a police officer was income. I had not fully realized the increased salary I had the potential to make in the corporate arena. This made the change of direction in profession that much easier to transition into and fueled my drive to be successful that much more. Upon graduation from Ferris, I had the opportunity to open and work in a brand-new store in West Michigan. Target was opening a new market on the western side of the state, and I was fortunate to be chosen to help open one of the Grand Rapids stores. What an exciting opportunity with beautiful stores, creating and developing new teams, a beautiful new apartment to call home and many new friends I would be making in the years to come. I could not wait to get going in this endeavor and make my mark in a new position with a progressive company leading the way in the retail industry. The future was looking bright.

FOUR

WHEN DESTINY MEETS DESTINATION

For I know the plans I have for you, says the Lord. They
are plans for good and not for disaster, to give you a
future and a hope.

—Jeremiah 29:11

The day I arrived at my new store in Grand Rapids, I was nervous, anxious and eager to start this next chapter in my life. I knocked on the security door and was met by my new area investigator. She opened the door with a giant smile and a warm handshake and said, "Hello, Michael! You've been highly recommended, and we can't wait for you to get started." After some small talk and a briefing about the store and surrounding area, it was time to get out and meet the team. This was the first weekend the store team was allowed into the building after construction had been completed.

We were beginning a power-packed weekend called 'Planorama,' where the new team would essentially assemble fixtures and set up the entire store. This first day included only those in leadership positions from our new store and supporting stores from our district. Experienced team members and leaders from many other stores from across the state were onsite and preparing to assist and train our new team. Beginning the following day, we would have hundreds of team members working fast and furiously to accomplish an enormous workload. Working from the back to the front, there would not be any corner of the building left untouched. By the time the weekend was over, we would be ready to start receiving merchandise and supplies to fill our entire building. We had one month to have the store completed, fully stocked and teams trained and ready to open before we started to receive our guests. Time to head out and meet some of the people I would now be working with. I did not know it at the time, but one of those first team members I would meet would later become my wife and the reason why I consider myself to be the luckiest man alive. I remember it like it was yesterday. I was walking down the aisle in the middle of the store, heading toward what would become the women's department. She was with her immediate supervisor, assembling fixtures and preparing the walls and floor pad to receive all the new merchandise which would soon arrive. I walked by and remembered saying to myself, *Holy cow! Who is that?* I stopped for a minute to chat and introduce myself to them both. I then continued on to meet more people and to let them get back to their tasks at hand. I would not be able to get the new girl, Shelly, out of my mind anytime soon.

There is incredible energy in a new store during Planorama. It is infectious. It is a loud, controlled chaos with many moving parts and people. The workload is immense and requires a high sense of urgency and strong work ethic from every person involved. There is a strong sense of accomplishment as the transformation of the store unfolds in a matter of hours. Everything is new and clean with the latest fixturing, signing and supplies the company has to offer. There is a buzz of excitement in the air and a level of pride and partnership forming which is unbeatable. Opening a new store can be an addiction. It is extremely hard work with long hours, but the rewards are immense. It was a completely different environment than the older stores I had been accustomed to working in. However, there was one thing which did not change and was a common denominator for any location I had experience in, and that was crime. Regardless of the city or location, type of company, new or old building, each unique situation fueled my purpose and strengthened my expertise. Internal and external theft and fraud would always exist and thus, there would be a need for someone like me to take care of it. This is when I first realized I needed to be careful what I asked for.

One phenomenal opportunity which presented itself when opening a new market was the opportunity of promotion. New store markets are very fast-paced and fluid, producing much movement in positions for people, opening the door for promotion. Being young, fresh out of college and at the beginning of my career, I was focused on becoming a salaried leader in Target as quickly as possible. My current assignment was going to be tough and quite the challenge, so I was ready to get busy and do what I did best. From behind the scenes, my job was to enhance profits without becoming a liability. Detect dishonesty while creating a strong, protective presence. One of my strengths lies in my communication style and how I connect with people. I am skilled at building partnerships and projecting key messages while inspiring people along the way. I work hard to make others understand their significance in the big-picture vision for the store, team or project. Being part of building a new store was exciting in this regard because most of the team members were new, open-minded and excited for what they were involved in. Most often people were willing to be part of any solution, not part of the problems. I was very effective at teaching and training, as well as I had a high skill level relating to theft and fraud resolution. These attributes did not go unnoticed. Soon after those Grand Rapids stores opened, I was offered a promotion into an executive position, which included leading the asset protection team in my own store in the area. Interestingly enough, Shelly was having a similar experience and would also be receiving an executive-level promotion in the same store I was being assigned to. We had no idea the depth of relationship and friendship we would soon forge.

This new location was a high-sales-volume store and would create many unique operational and security challenges. Working in the same store but in different divisions of the store, Shelly in operations and me in security, we sometimes did not see things eye to eye. This presented some problems and created the first tough 'moment' we had. Shelly and I still laugh about it today. We collided like two freight trains on the same track. We were both strong leaders in our areas of expertise. We were early into the holiday season and the pressure was on. My supervisors had made it clear every team member had to go through asset-protection orientation within their first ten days of employment or they could not work. This was a corporate policy. The company's standards were very high, and it was crucial that each team member had a clear understanding of the security practices and his/her role in executing those practices. Our problem arose when a group of new team members made it through the store orientation but missed the asset protection orientation and they were now working in their respective areas. Having enough team members to staff the store appropriately to handle the holiday business had been a challenge. The leadership team worked extremely hard to hire, train and get people working as soon as possible. If someone got caught between the cracks due to scheduling conflicts, it was common for that person to be put to work without going through my security orientation. The intention was that they would be rescheduled as soon as possible. It was a balancing act with many moving parts and people involved. This process was being monitored very closely by my boss at the district office. The pressure was on, and I was feeling the heat.

A group of the new team members who had missed my orientation were cashiers and were now working the registers on a busy evening. Shelly was the leader of the front-end team, and she was also working on this night. With a long list of the team members I needed to get through orientation, I decided to act. I proceeded out of the office and to the front lanes. The store was filled with shoppers and every checkout lane was full. I walked to the registers with cashiers who were on my list and one by one turned off their lane lights. I politely asked the customers to find another lane and then escorted my cashiers back to the training room. They saw it as a relieving break from the hectic crowds and I began to complete their orientation. I had a sense of relief thinking I would not receive another phone call from the district office, challenging me on my lack of training the team. Then, out of nowhere, it happened. There was a loud knock at the door, and it swung open. There stood Shelly with an angry look on her face. She was visibly upset. With fire in her eyes, she aggressively pointed at me and professionally waved me into the hallway. She wanted to spare the cashiers from this moment of frustration. I had made a very bad decision which seriously interrupted the general operation of the business, and she challenged me and asked, "What were you thinking?" Needless to say, our professional relationship did not start off on the right foot. We would find this would not be the first of our differences of style and opinion in the workplace. Even though the store continued to present many challenges, Shelly and I would find a way to forge a professional relationship and become great partners in working toward common goals.

As time progressed, we found our rhythm with our store team to create a beautiful and profitable store. We all worked hard, and the efforts paid off. Shelly and I were an integral part of this success. Soon, I was promoted and took on a multi-store responsibility. I now had two different stores to oversee. This new position was due to realignment and structure changes within the company. Although one store position was eliminated, it offered the opportunity for a promotion for someone else. I was thrilled to be that person offered this promotion. Shelly and I now worked in the same city and district, but we were no longer working out of the same store. We found our relationship deepening into a new level of friendship. Even though we were working many long and hard hours, friendships amongst co-workers from different stores were created and we all started gathering outside of work. We worked hard and we played hard. I had much respect for Shelly professionally and now I found it exciting to discover the personal side of her. She was extremely smart, funny, interesting and beautiful, and I enjoyed being around her. I was looking for someone who would love me for who I was and who would also share similar goals, ethics and dreams in life. Neither of us was looking for a personal relationship but over time, our friendship blossomed into something much deeper. We were two young professionals, out in the world trying to make a name for ourselves. We would discover that both of us travelled two different, yet similar, paths. Neither of us intended big box retail to be our career, but somehow that is where we landed. We knew we were there for a reason. Just maybe that reason was to meet each other and to become one special force together.

Opportunity would once again present itself. My immediate supervisor called and asked me for a favor. The store he wanted me to go to had some unique opportunities and needed strong leadership. The security manager in that location had just been fired for theft himself, and a store atmosphere had been created which many thought was beyond repair. That store had become part of our district due to realignment, and it had been previously operating under very different guidelines and standards. The store culture needed to be rebuilt, and this would not be easy. If I took on this challenge, I would be taking on not only this store but also another. I would continue my multi-store responsibilities. A benefit was I would be closer to home and living in Wolverine Country – Ann Arbor, Michigan. After taking a weekend to consider my options, I decided this was a move for me. By this time, Shelly and I were dating more seriously, and we began to see very clearly a future together. We did not want to put distance between us in our blossoming relationship. But Shelly had also been promoted again and was being transferred to another store as well. Her new store was in a new city but one a bit closer to where I would now be working. We felt these moves were a sign for us to be together and strengthened our belief that if you work hard the company will take care of you. My dad had tried to warn me of living by this philosophy and to always remember life is short. At that time, I had no idea how significant this piece of advice would be for me in my future.

I knew my new store was a high-sales-volume location, but I had no idea what I was walking into. The team turnover was the worst in the chain, and the leadership team I was joining had a reputation for making bad decisions regarding the well-being of those on their team. It was one of those stores which was lacking leadership. My strategy was to treat people well and to provide positive reinforcement where I could while being purposeful when enforcing company standards. There were good people in this store, and I discovered that all they were looking for was someone to say 'thank you.' A simple 'hello' and sharing a genuine appreciation for the well-being of another went a long way. I discovered how culture and atmosphere played a big role in the healing process of a broken environment. This store reminded me why I had become interested in law enforcement in the first place—I wanted to help people and make a difference in the lives of others. Working in Ann Arbor also gave me the opportunity to strengthen my skills in building community partnerships. This was the first community in which I became closely involved and built strong partnerships with community leaders and local law enforcement. Together, we worked on various initiatives to provide a more safe and enjoyable place to live and work. I had a tremendous amount of personal and professional growth during my time spent in this store.

Retail was not easy, and we often sacrificed family time and holidays in the pursuit of our career goals. We were caught up in the corporate vacuum trading hours for money. With a lot on our plates, we decided we needed a break. Some fresh air and a little time away. So, we packed up and headed south. Our exact destination was undecided, but we were headed to North Carolina, knowing we would land on the beach at the ocean. Armed with a trusty oversized atlas, we mapped out our journey with a game plan of following major routes until we hit the water. With roughly 800 miles to explore, we loaded up the vehicle and we were on our way. The one specific destination in our plans was Cary, North Carolina, where our friends and my old boss, Mike Bruce, and his family lived. We were excited and could not wait to leave the everyday retail grind behind and get our toes into the sand.

We had an incredible trip, creating wonderful memories along the way. We could not believe how friendly people were the farther south we went. We were so impressed with one waiter in a breakfast restaurant we stopped at in Asheville that we left him a $20 tip. Our bill was less than $10. As planned, we stopped to spend some time with Mike and his wife, April, in Cary before making our way toward the coast. We drove until we were at the water. This happened to be in the Wilmington area, in Wrightsville Beach. The road ended in a parking lot next to the pier. On our left were a restaurant and the entrance to the pier. On our right was a hotel. In front of us was the beach and the ocean. Ahhh… heaven! One would think we would have already had a hotel room booked, but Shelly and I played by our own rules. Sometimes you just need to let life happen. We walked into the hotel and booked a room for that night. Then we went to explore. Most people from Michigan have a simple goal—get to the ocean.

Feeling our toes in the sand while walking on the beach and breathing in the ocean air was exhilarating. It was exactly what we needed. The next day we were fresh and eager for a day at the beach. We got up early and went for a long walk. As we walked, we spotted a distinct and unusual condo complex right on the beach. The design of the building had the oceanfront rooms coming to a V-point with triangular balconies and floor-to-ceiling windows for a spectacular view. We had to check this place out. We went in and inquired about any vacancies with an oceanfront room. Sure enough, a beautiful place was available, and we snatched it up. We quickly left to check out of the first hotel and move to our new special spot we would call home for the next five days. What a gift!

The beach and condo were incredible. We had a spectacular time and we quickly fell in love with coastal North Carolina. Being away from the stress and hustle of retail was exactly what we needed. We walked, talked, laughed and just simply enjoyed each other and our time alone. We loved the beauty and awe of Lake Michigan, but this was something more. There was something special about the ocean. We would sleep with our balcony doors cracked. Listening to the sounds of the waves gently lapping the beach lulled us into a sound sleep each night. We would awake to the sounds of the seagulls, calling out as they swooped overhead looking for their choice meal. The beauty of the sun peeking into the room and calling for us to come out and explore the day. The warmth of the air enveloped us as we walked along the beach with the sand sifting between our toes. Despite it being the end of September, the days were warm and humid and the nights pleasant, without the intense humidity of the summer. The stars were magnificent in the black of night, soothing and calming to end our days. We could not have dreamed of a better vacation and truly did not want it to end. We knew we had to get back to work in Michigan, but both Shelly and I dreamed of how fantastic it would be if we could call North Carolina home. We left this beautiful state with that dream etched into our minds.

Seizures would factor into my life once again and in a frightening way. As we made our way home filled with excitement, we were completely entranced by the beauty of our drive, especially in the mountains. It was a thrill to drive on the windy, hilly highway which wrapped itself around and through the Great Smoky Mountains. It was my turn to drive, and it was a rush cruising with the traffic racing through the curves. In a section with two lanes on our side of the highway, the mountains on our right were almost close enough to touch. On our left was a major drop-off and an incredible vista which seemed to stretch to infinity. It was a gorgeous day with the sun warming us through the windows and the blue sky dusted with light, wispy clouds. We were jamming to our tunes playing in the background, sometimes singing along and sometimes in conversation about our fabulous vacation. I felt like an Indy race car driver as I swerved around the bends with semitrailers passing us on the downhills and us passing them on the uphills. I was driving in the right lane of traffic. Shelly was looking out the window at the gorgeous scenery and enjoying the drive. As we were moving into a downhill section around a curve, she felt the car start to slow down. Looking over she asked me why I was slowing down. I didn't answer. Studying my face for a moment, suddenly a terrifying reality hit her. I was having a seizure! Shelly knew of my seizure diagnosis, but she had never witnessed me having one. Thankfully we were driving her car, which had a manual transmission. Having no time to figure out what to do, she acted on instinct. She immediately put the hazards on and started moving over the center console as she took control of the wheel. She tried to put her left leg over my legs to reach the brake but couldn't quite make it. She grabbed the stick shift and threw the car into neutral. Now we were drifting downhill, winding through curves with semis breathing down our back. Her heart was racing but she kept her nerves in control. As soon as the car was moving slowly enough, she tried to maneuver the car to the shoulder of the road as it appeared. We were approaching an emergency exit for runaway semitrailers. Thankfully this appeared because prior to this, the shoulder was not wide enough for us to stop safely. We thankfully reached a point where we were off the road far enough and we were going slow enough to safely pull the emergency brake. She slowly pulled the brake, and the car finally came to a halt. Shelly sat there for a few minutes trying to catch her breath and to slow her heart rate down. I was still in my seizure and not in full consciousness. It took about four more minutes for me to come back to reality. I was confused, looking around wondering why we had stopped on the side of the road. It took me a while to remember where we were and what we had been doing. Once Shelly realized I was ok and back to full consciousness, we both got out of the car. We needed to vent some energy and try to process what had just happened. Shelly burst into tears once she got out of the car. She was shaking and pacing, working out that extra energy. As she relayed what had just happened, I was stunned. How could I have gone into a seizure during a time when I was feeling so great? I was happy, enjoying life and having a blast with my love. I had never had a seizure at such a critical time before. This was an identifying moment in our lives and in our relationship. This would be a moment etched into our memories forever. But this terrifying experience did not slow me down.

Returning home in the beginning of October, we could not get our trip out of our minds. As soon as we returned to our stores, we started talking about how much we loved the Carolinas and would jump at any opportunity to help open stores in that region. We became aware of the company expansion plan to open at least 250 new stores on the East Coast in the coming years. We both made it known to our supervisors that we wanted to be considered for those soon-to-be East Coast stores. We specifically targeted North Carolina. Stores were planned to open there the following March, and they would need experienced leaders to help open the market successfully. It did not take long to get the call. By week one of December, we were heading south for interviews. Our destination: Raleigh-Durham, North Carolina. In mid-January of 1995, we found ourselves moving to Raleigh.

Officially we were now 'Gone to Carolina,' singing this favorite James Taylor song all the way there.

FIVE

A LONG DARK ROAD

*So do not fear, for I am with you; do not be dismayed, for
I am your God. I will strengthen you and help you; I will
uphold you with my righteous right hand.*

— *Isaiah 41:10*

Our transfer happened so quickly we actually left Michigan before
our belongings did. My sister Mary would be handling the final packing
and loading of our items a few days later when the movers arrived to trans-
port our furnishings. We were leaving my car behind to be towed with the
moving truck and we had Shelly's car loaded to the brim. Standing in the
driveway with tears flowing, we hugged Mary as we said our last goodbyes.
It was so hard to believe this was it. We had had a wonderful Warner family send-off with the entire family gathering for a final goodbye two nights
before. We spent the time together laughing, sharing stories, cracking jokes

and discussing the future in true Warner form. My mom had created a photo album capturing so many wonderful memories and moments of our lives in Michigan. She was so clever she drew a map of the United States on the cover, highlighting the trek we would be following from Michigan to North Carolina. It was priceless and precious, and we planned to add pictures to it as we began our new life in North Carolina. Brimming with excitement, we grabbed our kitty, Kiki, hugged Mary and headed south. Shelly decided to drive the first leg of the trip as we planned to share the responsibility for driving between the two of us. It was a beautiful sunny day. Kiki was finally settled in and curled up in the back seat for a nap, and we buzzed with excited conversation for what was ahead. As we left the border of Michigan and headed into Ohio, little did we know things would not go as smoothly as we expected.

Back in those days, we listened to not only the radio but also cassette tapes. We had one of those big, clunky cases to house the many cassettes of our favorite artists and it was sitting behind the driver's seat. Because Shelly was driving, she asked me to reach back and grab the case so we could put on some new music. As I reached back and behind her seat, I felt instant pain shoot into my shoulder. It was so severe I just fell into Shelly's lap, holding my arm and screaming in agony. At first she laughed because she thought I was playing around. "What are you doing?" she asked through giggles. "Just drive," I told her, not moving from my position. "What's going on?" she asked. "Are you having a heart attack or something?" At first I couldn't even answer because I was in so much pain. She started to get really scared not knowing what was happening. I finally was able to sit back in my seat, but I continued to hold my arm/shoulder and moan in agony. I told her I thought I would soon be ok and to just keep driving.

When it was easier for me to speak, I shared with her that I had an old shoulder injury from playing hockey in my youth and I thought I had just dislocated my shoulder. Watching me with concern, she started to look for an exit ramp to pull off the highway. In one of the many blessings we would have throughout our lives, we realized the next exit had signs indicating it was also a hospital exit. God was with us. We pulled into the parking lot of the hospital and leaving Kiki in the car, we entered through the emergency room entrance. I was immediately taken back for care. Shelly was not a fan of hospitals and quickly became queasy from the smells. "I'll be outside and will check back soon to see how he is doing," she told a nurse. After her initial inquiry to check on me, she realized we would be there a couple of hours due to the heavy pain medication they had put me on. They had reset my shoulder, but I still needed to be monitored for at least an hour before they would release me to ensure I did not have any adverse side effects. Now what was she supposed to do with Kiki in the car? It was time for a walk. She drove to a nearby pet store and bought him a leash. This was a first for our kitty, as he was an indoor cat and not allowed to roam outside. It must have been a funny sight to witness Shelly walking this striking pure white cat with piercing blue eyes down the street with a leash. Only she could think of that! She walked him around the hospital grounds for over an hour while waiting for me, checking periodically to ensure I was ok. Once I was released from the hospital with my arm in a sling and loopy from medication, we loaded back into the car with Shelly at the wheel again. Unfortunately, she would now have to be the driver for the entire trip. This was going to be a long drive.

Kiki sat in the window sunning himself all the way to North Carolina. He loved it and was a great passenger. He was quite the piece of eye candy for passing motorists as they drove past us. It was funny to watch their expressions once they noticed him in the window. Other than a few tense moments from Shelly due to fatigue of driving, the rest of the trip was uneventful. We just wanted to make it safely to our destination. We drove straight through and arrived in the Durham area late that night. Exhausted, we decided to get a hotel for the evening and would finish our final short leg of the trip the next morning. We fell into a deep sleep as soon as we hit the bed. The next day, we made it to our new apartment, unloaded our car and the limited belongings we had travelled with and started to settle in. Fortunately, we did not have to report to our stores for two more days, so we were able to rest, check out the area and allow my shoulder to do some healing.

Our first day in our respective stores was also the first day of Planorama. Luckily we had experience with this, as it was a crazy time for us to start with our new teams. We felt we were behind the eight ball because we had not been involved with the planning process for this critical weekend, but we quickly fell into place and got to work. It turned out to be a perfect weekend to meet so many people so quickly. We were the newbies and had yet to establish ourselves with our co-workers. The long days of hard work quickly turned into weeks, and before we knew it, the week of our soft opening was upon us. Four new stores would be opening at the same time: Raleigh, Cary, Rocky Mount and Myrtle Beach, South Carolina. People in all these communities were bursting at the seams for us to open. The energy, excitement and expectation for Target to be opening stores in this new market were all electrifying. Team members were proud of their work and could not wait to share the store with their friends and families. Each store was gearing up for what we called 'VIG (Very

Important Guests) Night'. That was an evening of celebration for our teams as we opened our doors for the first time to family, friends and the media during our ribbon-cutting ceremony. The following day would begin our quiet opening experience where we would be open to the public for business, but we were not yet advertising that. Sales and guest traffic were historically low and slow during the period, as the general public was not yet aware we were open. The advertised date for opening was the upcoming Friday. This slower period of shopping traffic typically helped our stores to get into a true rhythm of routine and operation so new team members could hone their skills before the onslaught of Grand Opening Weekend. 'Slow' is a relative term however, and these new markets were not going to give us much of a cushion for this training period. Word travelled quickly that we were open, and the game was on as people from our communities started flocking to the stores. Unfortunately, we did not have time to take a bit of a break from the long days and hours we had already spent to get the stores ready to open. That was only the precursor for the main event. It was time to rock 'n' roll!

Grand Opening Day was Friday, March 17, 1995. It was so busy; it was like a rock concert in the stores. From the moment we opened our doors in the morning to the last guest leaving the store in the evening, we were running. Our days started hours before the doors opened as we stocked our merchandise and performed all of the tasks needed in preparation for business. And the work did not stop at closing time. We still had hours of work after that last guest had left the building to finish putting the store back together after the day's business and to perform all the closing duties needed to end the day. It took hundreds of team members to make this happen, let alone all the planning and preparation necessary for them to do their jobs effectively. The days were exhausting and endless. But we were having a blast, amazed at how busy each of our stores was. We were some of the highest performing sales volume stores in the company, and we were competing against each other to see who could be at the top. It was awesome and a bit insane. We found ourselves getting up in the wee hours of the morning, heading into work and working easily 15–18-hour days, only to head home for a few hours of sleep and turn around and do it again the next day. We were young and running on adrenaline and had a drive to be the best and to enjoy every moment of it. Shelly and I saw very little of each other in those weeks, but when we were not at our stores, we spent every minute together. We knew this routine was temporary and we would settle down eventually, but we were grateful to be a part of it at the time.

Our apartment was in Raleigh, closer to the store Shelly worked at. I had nearly an hour's commute to my store in Rocky Mount. I had my hands full with theft scenarios right from the beginning. My store was located just off an exit from I-95, near the NC/VA border. I-95 is a known traffic route of criminal activity running from Florida straight up to the Northeast. This provided that criminal element of people an opportunity to steal from businesses close to the interstate and then quickly escape the area by getting back on it. I was ready for this challenge though. I was impressed with the level of technology and the resource package Target provided for me to do my job effectively. I had the newest and best cameras, CCTVs, monitors and more. The team I had developed for asset protection in my store was experienced and now well trained. We were a well-oiled machine ready to protect our team, our guests and the assets of our store. I had already established a strong rapport with local law enforcement and a good working relationship with nearby retailers. We would do our best to send a strong message to criminals that Target was not the place for them.

It was Monday night, March 20, 1995, and we had just ended our Grand Opening weekend. Both Shelly and I were still working late into the evening after many long, grueling hours in the past days. The opening of our new stores was going well, but we were exhausted, and I could not wait to get on the road. Just as I was preparing to leave the store for my hour's commute home, there was a loud knock at the door. I put down my briefcase and opened the door. A friendly stocky man stood in the doorway and introduced himself. He said, "Hi! I'm your neighbor from across the street. I'm the district security manager and have been intending to come over to introduce myself. Is this a bad time?" I would not be going home yet. Although his timing was not ideal, I was very interested in talking to this leader from our competitor who held a position in the same division as me. The district manager was very professional, and I was happy to meet someone that could give me additional insight about the community and some of the details that could help me build an even stronger security team than I already had. Suddenly, I realized how late it was and politely ended our conversation. I had a long drive ahead of me, and the only thing on my mind now was getting home to Shelly. Just before leaving the store, I called home and discovered she too was not yet home. So, I left a message on our answering machine and headed for the door. It was just after midnight as I headed to my car.

Shortly into my drive on that dark rural highway, I approached a part of the interstate with a slight bend leading onto an overpass going over railroad tracks. I was settled in, driving around 70 mph, as my mind wandered to getting home to my sweetheart. Something caught my eye and the next thing I remember was my car moving sideways as it was scraping against the guardrail. Dirt and smoke were rushing through the car and I was disoriented. *What was I looking at? Why am I not seeing out of my windshield?* I realized I was lying back in my seat, and I must have been looking at the ceiling in my car. As the car bounced along something hard and uneven, I tried to pump my brakes to stop the car. For some reason I could not do this. The car started to slow down, and I could not tell which direction I was facing. Finally, the car came to a stop. I had no idea where I was or what had happened to me. I tried to look around but all I saw was darkness as I heard the hissing of my engine and the smoke settled around me. With so many strange smells I could not recognize, and an inability to move from where I lay, the darkness worked to overcome me. I began to pray. Without hesitation I began repeating, "I'm going to be alright. I love my Shelly, I love my Shelly, I love my Shelly...." It was as if I knew Shelly was my reason to live. What felt like only minutes later, one of the first blessings of the night appeared. A bright light was now shining into my face and a stern voice said, "You're going to be okay, partner. We've got you from here." With emergency lights flashing all around in the darkness, I started to feel a sense of calm and peace come over me. I could feel I was in good hands. What I did not yet realize was how much my life had just changed in an instant. What I *did* know? Our Creator was in control. I felt completely calm with this realization. I continued to pray to God to help and protect me. I also felt an intense level of love and longing for Shelly. I continued my chant, "I love my Shelly, I love my Shelly." I could not move, but I felt a strong, comfortable presence around me. With so many flashing lights and the sounds of many people echoing around me, I knew there was a large emergency response. I asked the first officer who had spoken to me if I had hit a deer. With a strange look on his face he replied, "Oh no partner, you hit cows. Black Angus cows."

The call had gone into 911 from a passerby. A driver had been traveling east on route US 64 around midnight when she had noticed cows in the road on the opposite side of the highway. Emergency responders had already been dispatched to the area when my accident occurred. This quick response would be a crucial element to my outcome. With a complete level of professionalism, a team of unsung heroes began to work. The priority was to get me out of the car and to stabilize my neck to prevent further damage. At the same time, others were working fast to secure the accident scene and to ensure it was safe from other traffic and concerned onlookers. They quickly, yet carefully, loaded me into the ambulance, and with sirens blaring, we went screaming off into the blackness of the night toward the hospital. Their wisdom, expertise and level of care would be major factors in the determination of the extent of my injury. I was lying flat on a wooden board as first responders worked feverishly, busily checking my vitals and trying to stabilize me. The interior lights of the ambulance were so bright they were not only blinding to me but also highlighted the intensity on the faces of my caregivers. They were poking and prodding me, asking, "Can you feel this? How about this?" They were working hard to carefully evaluate the extent of my injury. Surprisingly I had very little feeling, but I do recall a sharp pain in the lower back. Later it would be discovered that the pain in my back was coming from my handcuffs from work. My badge and handcuffs were in my back pocket. As I lay on the wooden board, they were being pushed into me and digging into my lower spine. I had small lacerations on my face and arms and would later discover a cut on my foot, all from the windshield which had shattered into a million pieces. It was amazing I did not have more visible wounds based on the condition my car was in when they had arrived on the scene. I would soon come to find out more details regarding the accident itself. The impact when I hit the cows was so severe that my driver's seat had reclined. Unbeknownst to me, when I hit the cows, one actually landed on my car. It landed on the hood, windshield and roof of the car and crushed the entire front end like tinfoil. Although the seat reclining on impact was a safety feature of the vehicle, which actually saved my life, the movement of the seat was a fraction too slow. When the cow landed, the roof of the car just happened to catch the top of my head and snapped my neck as it caved in before the seat reclined. The cow weighed 1,500 lb. Thank goodness the car I was driving was a Mercury Cougar. That car was a tank and it had saved my life in this freak accident. This was another blessing in my life. Just that day, Monday, I had put down a deposit on a new car I planned to buy. I was supposed to be trading in my Mercury on the upcoming Friday in order to purchase a new Mitsubishi Eclipse. If I had been driving the Eclipse, I would never have survived the accident. Another blessing? I was later told that the movement I felt while the car was still in motion was from it bouncing along the guardrail of the overpass. That guardrail also saved my life. If I had gone through it, my car would have careened over the edge of the overpass and onto the train tracks below. With a 1,500-lb cow along for the ride on the hood, I can't imagine I would have survived that fall. There were so many miracles already working for me that night. But getting back to me in the back of that ambulance? I was just trying to stay conscious and keep my wits about me. Without fully understanding what was happening, I remember thinking, *Holy Cow! What just happened?*

Cows. Traveling on the highway. How in the world does this happen? The path the cows had travelled was itself a major part of the story, one that someone from the city of Detroit would never believe. Taking into consideration that I had never even ridden a horse; I would have never believed that I would later be dubbed 'The Cowboy' and the butt of many jokes relating to livestock. Many of these jokes I created myself. Long after the accident, I spent much time watching people while they ate at their favorite restaurants. I have often joked that the emblem of my Mercury Cougar was embedded in that steak on their plate. I would think to myself, *Could it be from one of my cows?*

The cows are believed to have travelled from the south side of the road to the north side. The multiple sets of hoof prints leading away from the fence along the highway were the first and most visible sign where they escaped from the pasture. It was later discovered that the fence had been cut with wire cutters and the area had pedestrian foot traffic visible on the ground. It was also discovered that this was not the first time that cattle from the same farm had escaped through the hole in the fence. On a few other occasions, according to surrounding neighbors, the cattle were seen roaming around on other people's property and some neighbors had helped return them to the pasture with the reassurance that the fence would later be fixed and maintained. From the initial investigation and findings, it was certainly plausible that the cattle escaped from the south side of the service road, crossed the service road and travelled through the opening of the highway fence to get into the limited-access area of U.S. 64. It was discovered that they travelled a quarter of a mile east along U.S. 64 from the point they entered the right-of-way (my side of the road). The area of the collision had very limited access in that it was enclosed on both sides by highway guardrails. The initial impact was on a bridge on U.S. 64 which went up and over train tracks. Two cows died in the accident. One was buried at the scene the next day by the county animal control officer with help from the Department of Transportation. The other cow was too big and had to be towed with the vehicle on which it had landed. Other cows were seen running back to the hole in the fence where the farm's caretaker and two local landowners assisted in getting them back into the pasture. What could those cows have been thinking as they raced back to the safety of the pasture and the farm? It's amazing to think they knew where to go!

SIX

YOU PEOPLE NEED
A REALITY CHECK

When I am afraid, I put my trust in you.

—Psalm 56:3

What is that noise? The phone can't be ringing again! Am I dreaming? That must be the alarm center again. How many alarm calls have I taken in the past week? I told myself I was *not* answering the phone at that time. I had only gotten a handful of hours of sleep over the past four days. *I am so tired. I am going to let someone else take this call. They can call the next person on the list.* These were my thoughts as I tried to pull out of my slumber. I had not made it home from work until after midnight and I had gone into work very early that morning. Michael was still not home. I had walked into the house after getting home from work, heard his message from the machine that he was on the way home, and I had sat on the edge of the bed and fallen back. Immediately I fell asleep on my back, fully dressed as my legs hung over the end of the bed. Now it was possible I had to answer another alarm call. I heard our answering machine kick in and I heard an authoritative voice. It was definitely the alarm center. *Not again!* As I moved awake, I heard the voice say: "So, can you please call nurse so-and-so at Nash General Hospital as soon as you get this message?" Immediately I was wide awake and running for the phone.

"Hello? This is Shelly. Are you still there?"

"Hi, Shelly. I am calling from Nash General Hospital. We have Michael Warner here and he has been in a car accident. We need you to come to the hospital as soon as possible. Are you able to come?"

"Yes! Definitely. Can I speak to him?"

"Well… he is with the nurse right now, but if you would like to hold—"

"No! That is ok. I am on the way! It will take me about an hour to get there."

I ran out of the room, grabbed my wallet and keys and rushed out of the door. On the near-hour-long drive it took me to get there, so many thoughts rushed through my head. I did not get enough information from the nurse. I should have asked more questions. *How badly was he hurt? Was anyone else involved in the accident? Were they hurt? What if someone else had died?* All of those thoughts and more were rushing through my mind as I raced to the hospital. The night was black with very few stars out. I had already made it to US 64 and it was nearly deserted. Darn! I noticed I needed gas and had to pull over to fill up my tank. The first open gas station I found was an old one in a rural area. Mine was the only car there, the night was pitch black with few lights around me and I had to go inside to pay. The guy working there looked at me and could tell I had been crying. He tried to chitchat with me and was curious about what was wrong with me. When I told him I had to get to the hospital, as my boyfriend had been in a car accident, he tried to come around the counter and give me a hug. "No, thanks," I said quickly and ran out of the store to my car. *What the heck!* I thought to myself. *Creep!* I just needed to get back on the road. When I arrived at the hospital, the parking lot was nearly empty. It was an eerie feeling walking through a nearly empty parking lot of an emergency entrance at a hospital in the middle of the night. Fear, worry, concern and uneasiness coursed through my body. As I entered the hospital, I was met at the doors by a uniformed police officer. "Are you Shelly?" he asked. "Yes, I am," I responded. "Before you go in, there is something you need to know."

I thought I was in a state of shock. My heart was racing. It was surreal, standing in the emergency waiting room entrance with a police officer who met me at the door. Does that always happen? Why was he waiting for me at the door? He stated he needed to share something with me before I went back to see Michael. My heart started racing even faster. This could not be good. He told me Michael had been in a traumatic car accident and the doctors were actively working on him at that moment. Slowly he said, "You need to know Michael has suffered a spinal cord injury and they are about to put him in a halo." *What?!* My heart sank and the world went quiet. All I could hear was the beating of my heart and buzzing in my ears. I had one instantaneous thought racing through my mind: *Michael is paralyzed.*

As the officer led me toward the swing doors leading to the emergency room area, I noticed a man out of the corner of my eyes. He was dressed in boots, coveralls and a flannel shirt. He had started to approach me. He was crying and apologizing over and over. "I'm so sorry," he said through tears. "I didn't know. I was trying to get there," he continued on. Who was this guy and why was he trying to talk to me? He was waving the hat in his hands and desperately trying to connect with me. I had no idea who he was, nor did I have any interest in talking to him. I can remember the sorrow, confusion and fear from the information I had just received about Michael. Now I was angry at this intrusion to this moment from a stranger. I feel a bit bad about my behavior now, but then I just looked at him in confusion, put my hand up and said to him, "I don't know you and I can't talk to you right now." I continued with the officer. I would later find out the gentleman was the caretaker of the farm from which the cows had escaped. He was devastated about the accident and obviously struggling with some very strong emotions himself. But I was not the one to comfort him. Approaching the swing doors, all I could hear was laughter. And Michael's voice in the middle of it. *What is going on? Why are people laughing? What could possibly be funny in this situation?* I felt like I was in a Monty Python movie or something. *Am I dreaming?* But sadly, I was not. As I entered the room, there was Michael, amid a team of medical personnel, talking and sharing something which was making everyone laugh. When he looked over and saw me, he said, "There's my Shelly. Hi, Honey!" I took in the scene of Michael smiling and all the doctors and nurses smiling with him. There was a crazy contraption hanging above his head. It looked like something out of the movie *Frankenstein*. It was made of metal, circular with two levels of rings and had screws on four sides of it. The moment was surreal and one which is seared into my brain forever. I ran over, touched his face and gave him a kiss. Tears flowing from my eyes, I said to him, "I love you, Honey! You are going to be ok. You are in good hands with these doctors. You are going to be ok!" I stared into his eyes, and we spoke for just a bit before I was ushered back out so the medical team could continue what they needed to do for him. I struggled leaving him and walking away. All I wanted to do was stay with him. I was so afraid and felt so alone. *What is going to happen to him? What if that wonderful sense of humor and wonderful smile he has disappeared? What if I don't see him again? What am I supposed to do now?*

As I walked back out into the waiting room with the police officer, a doctor and a nurse joined us. The doctor asked me to join him in a consultation room. As our little group started walking toward that door, another man joined us. He was wearing all black with a white collar at his neck. As soon as I saw him, my heart dropped again. The panic running through me must have been obvious on my face, as they rushed to keep me standing. The doctor immediately tried to calm me down and reassure me the pastor who was joining us was there purely for my support. My first thought when I saw him was that Michael was going to die. All I knew of emergency room situations was from what I had watched on TV. Every time a pastor or a priest entered the picture, their purpose was to give the patient their last rites. I have no idea how I did not pass out. I was shaking from head to toe as my nervous system was on an overdrive and adrenaline was coursing through my veins. As we all sat down in a tiny room, the doctor began to share with me the extent of Michael's injuries and what the next steps in procedures were going to be. He asked many questions about us, Michael's health history and more. Technically I was not the decision maker, as Michael and I were not yet married. We were not even officially engaged yet. Obviously, I needed to call Michael's family, especially his mom, to let them know what had happened, but it was urgent I do it now to get proper authorization from his mom, Susan, for his treatment. It was now about

3:30 a.m. and I hated the idea of making this call to her in the middle of the night. The thought of her hearing her phone ring at that hour made me even more emotional. I imagined how it was going to frighten her. Taking deep breaths to calm my nerves before making the call, I tried desperately to keep my own emotions in check. I did not want to make the situation worse when we spoke. As soon as I heard Susan answer the phone, the tears immediately started to flow. As I failed in my struggle to keep my emotions at bay, I heard Susan's voice change. She moved so quickly from a sound of confusion and worry at receiving a phone call in the middle of the night to one of strength and power as she tried to take control of whatever it was she was about to hear. As I began to share the situation through my sobs, Susan spoke calmly, clearly and with control and asked if she could speak to the doctor. She took a quick moment to grab a pen and paper and then I handed the phone over. Gratefully, the doctor took control of the situation and was able to share the facts and details of what Michael was facing due to his injuries. At the end of the call, I took the phone back and Susan offered me calm and reassuring words. I could only fathom what that must have felt like, to be a mother states away and receive a phone call like that in the middle of the night. She is a strong, beautiful, powerful woman who continues to exude that strength today, even in moments of crisis. Maybe even more so during those moments. She told me she would be making plans to get down to North Carolina as soon as she could. I could not wait to have her come and share that message with Michael as well. She also told me to tell the doctors we were engaged so that I would become the decision maker for Michael as needed.

In the accident, Michael's fifth vertebra had broken into pieces and now his spine was out of alignment. The first procedure needing to be done immediately was to re-establish normal spine alignment by putting him into traction. They put him into a halo. I am not sure if you are familiar with what a halo is, but it is scary! The halo is a brace that permits absolutely no movement of the head, neck and upper torso. It is made of large metal bars which are drilled and screwed into a patient's head in four different spots. Something kind of astonishing we discovered while writing this book was the spots on Michael's skull where the halo had been secured. He started shaving his head completely this year as we were writing this book. One day I looked more closely at a couple of spots on his skull, which I had noticed once he started shaving his head. "Let me look more closely at your head," I said to him. "You need to check out these spots in the mirror. I think they might be scars from where they screwed the halo into your head." Now, we realized these were exactly that. They were the scars from when he had to wear the halo. Almost 26 years later we were discovering this! That's incredible.

Once they were able to stabilize Michael, they moved him to a room in the ICU. I relocated to the ICU waiting room and found my spot I would move into for many days ahead. I can still picture to this day the placement of my chair, against the wall and facing the doors. It was a hard, light wood chair frame with cranberry fabric seat cushions. I remember the color of the carpet had that same cranberry color in a continuous pattern mixed with hues of cream, beige and black. The wallpaper covering the walls was a different pattern of similar hues of cream and beige and accented the carpet and chairs. It was very tastefully done. I am sure it was designed to be a backdrop of comfort offered to help calm and soothe nerves and emotions. When I looked at it, I felt nothing. I felt numb. But I remember it. I remember the sound of the TV droning on in the background and me being irritated by it. Most of all, I remember the spot on the wall I would just stare at during and in between my endless prayers. Do you ever do that? Stare at something, looking directly at it but not actually seeing it? My memory is of time standing still. Like the world had just stopped. At least my world had. Why is it we feel closer than ever to God during moments of crisis? For me, that realization is in knowing He is the only ONE who has ultimate control over what happens. He provides that comfort and sense of calm we all desperately need in those moments. I was grateful for His presence and my faith in Him. I may have been physically by myself in that waiting room, but I was not alone. Even though Michael and I were not yet married, the hospital staff treated me like I was his immediate family. They would allow me to see Michael for short periods during visiting hours even though hospital rules allowed only immediate family to do that. They knew we had plans to marry, and they also knew we had only been in the Carolinas for a couple of months with both of our families still in Michigan. The only people we knew in the area were the people we worked with, and we had only known them for less than two months. God had graced us with one friend in the area whom we knew from Michigan. His name is Mike Bruce, and he and his family lived nearby. He would come to be a very important person and support to me during this crisis, and he was for Michael as well.

Later that morning, I had to drive home to get key items needed for us at the hospital. When I had left the apartment the night before, I was not thinking clearly, and I had only grabbed my wallet and keys. I had nothing else with me. So, I needed to return home, feed our kitty, gather the things I would need for the hospital and make the necessary phone calls to all of the key people and our bosses at work. Another one of the first people I called was Mike Bruce. When I returned to the hospital later that morning, Mike Bruce would join me there and sit with me for hours in that waiting room. For multiple days on end, he would sit with me and keep me company, giving me strength. I could not have made it through that time without him. He will forever have a special place in my heart for his unselfish love and the friendship he offered to both me and Michael. God also graced him with a great sense of humor and a profound faith in Jesus. He knew just how to lighten my spirits and calm my soul through the most trying times. He is one of those people who will make you spit your drink out laughing; he is so funny. I was so grateful to have him by my side. In addition to this, I had an interesting thing happen to me on that first drive back to Raleigh. I still laugh about it today. I remember feeling like I was in a daze, operating as if I was in a fog. I have come to realize when you experience traumatic moments in your life, your senses become hyper alert. When I left the hospital that morning, I was struck by how beautiful the weather was and how intense the colors of the day were. The sky was so blue and the grass so green, it was almost blinding. The sun was high and bright, beaming warmth to me through the car windows. I was driving on the same divided highway Michael had been driving just a few hours before and I was lost in thought. Suddenly, I saw something out of the corner of my eye. I looked to my left and I could not believe my eyes. There, in the middle of the highway in the green grass of the median, lay a big black cow on its back with all four legs straight up in the air! I couldn't believe it. That was one of the cows Michael had hit! Just lying there, in the center of the highway like it were a normal thing to see. I don't know about you, but we were from the city. Cows on the highway was just not something we could have ever dreamed of witnessing ourselves. I could only shake my head and thank God Michael was still alive and that no one else had been injured in the accident. I wondered what happened to the other cows. *Did they all just run back home to the farm when they saw their friends get hit? Did they run away and were now wandering around, lost and confused and at risk of causing another accident?* So weird to think about.

When I made the necessary calls to the people at work, it was incredible how supportive and kind everyone was. Of course they were shocked to hear of the accident, and they immediately offered help and support to us both in any way we needed. I cannot say enough how incredible our leadership teams at Target were in support of both Michael and me. The outpouring of concern and help we received amazes us even today. We were blessed to be working with a team of very special people with huge hearts who treated us like family. When we use the phrase 'our Target family,' we mean it. That is just who the people we worked with at the time were. Looking back, it's interesting to think of. Here we were, at a time in our lives when our jobs and our careers were of utmost importance to us. We were deeply committed to our jobs and the company we worked for. We were having the time of our lives in the excitement of opening new stores in communities which could not get enough of our stores. We were young, inspired and striving to do great things in our careers. We had been spending the bulk of our hours and days trying to meet the demands of our jobs, and we were having a blast doing it. We were where we thought we were meant to be and grateful for it. It is interesting how quickly all of that changed for me in a flash. One moment, my thoughts, hours and days were consumed with work, and the next, none of that mattered. All that mattered was my Michael, who was lying paralyzed in the ICU. I became laser focused on him and barely left the ICU waiting room other than to visit him each hour and to use the restroom. I knew I should eat something—we all need sustenance to survive. But I could not stomach the thought of eating anything. It was a struggle just to go to the cafeteria to get coffee and stretch my legs. I could not stand the smell of it. It was so nauseating. It did not help that it was in the basement, the same floor as the morgue for the hospital. I hated going there, so I would get in and out as soon as I could and then return to my place, my chair, in the ICU waiting room. That is where I needed to be. For my Michael. I could not think too far ahead, as the future was so unknown and, honestly, very overwhelming. It is amazing how something like a severe car accident or crisis moment can make you rearrange your priorities in an instant. Not always do you keep those priorities straight for the long haul though. It is very easy to get them jumbled back up again.

Susan and Bob made it to the hospital Thursday night, two days after the accident. Mike Bruce was gracious enough to pick them up from the airport and bring them to the hospital. I cannot explain the feeling I had of seeing them in person. It was a huge sense of relief to know they were with me and could help us walk through the next crucial days of decision-making. The following day, on Friday, Michael would be undergoing surgery. That was a scary and nerve-wracking experience to think of what the potential outcome of this spinal surgery could be for Michael. Michael was so happy to see his mom and brother and I know it was such a relief for them to see him in person as well. What a lift in spirit for us all! Bob shared how he had been so worried and unsure how Michael would appear once they got to the hospital. He did not know what to think and felt very uncertain. Once they walked in and saw Michael and saw him smile at them and share his joy for them to be there, that worry dissipated immediately. It was a huge relief for them to see his spirit and character were still completely intact. It had a very calming effect on him, and it gave him comfort in knowing Michael would fight whatever was ahead for him. The power of Michael's spirit was shining through.

I sat for hours, day after day, talking to God and praying for Michael's recovery. I prayed about how we had been living our lives and where our priorities had been and how this experience was going to change us for the better. We already had so many blessings and I just knew our future would hold so many more. Our future was unknown, but with God, all things are possible. The next day, while Michael was in surgery, his mom, Bob and I sat in a surgery waiting room and we were discussing what was ahead for us both. Up to this point, not once did Michael speak of or think he would never walk again. These thoughts and words never came out of his mouth. In fact, it was truly remarkable to be witness to his experience. He stayed his true positive and forward-thinking self. He maintained his sense of humor and fun personality, and it was so refreshing just being near him. Watching him helped to calm us all and to shape our perspective. Because of this, we had all adopted the same attitude and thought process. We too believed he would walk again. That his life would not be confined to a wheelchair. At the time, we lived in a third-floor apartment in Raleigh, which did not have an elevator. As we were in the waiting room waiting to hear from the doctor the outcome of the surgery, we were discussing what was needed in the days ahead. I was sharing with Susan and Bob that I had already spoken to the management at our apartment complex about the probability of us needing to move into a handicap accessible apartment when Michael was ready to return home. Although we did not see him being wheelchair bound for the rest of his life, I did anticipate he would probably be coming home in a wheelchair for a period until he regained his ability to walk again. The doctor had walked into the room while I had been discussing this. The doctor had been sitting back, listening to us for a bit. Suddenly, he blurted out, "You people need a reality check! Michael will probably NEVER walk again!" Silence filled the room. It was like a boom of thunder had unleashed upon us. I was stunned. His outburst shocked me into silence. I was on the verge of a breakdown when I looked at Susan. She looked back at me for a moment and then slowly turned to the doctor. Fully composed and in complete control, she calmly but firmly stated to the doctor our belief was he would walk again and recover his mobility and because we felt strongly about that, that is how we were going to move forward with our plans. Paralysis has been the reality for many people, but we did not believe it was going to be ours. And if it did turn out to become our truth… well then, we would deal with that if/when that situation arose. Until then, this was how we were going to handle things. In that moment, she became my hero! She was AMAZING!!! And I was completely in awe of her composure and grace under pressure. I was sure glad she had it because at that moment, I did not. The doctor nodded and backed down on his communication style and then proceeded to share with us the outcome of the surgery for Michael and how he had done. The doctor was very pleased with how everything had gone. They had done a spinal fusion using a metal plate and part of Michael's hip to fuse into the C-5 area of his spinal column. There had been loose bone chips from damage to the fifth and sixth vertebrae and a 25% dislocation of the vertebrae. The fifth vertebra was the most badly damaged and the fusion now strengthened that area from the fourth vertebra down to the sixth. There was no permanent injury detected to the spinal cord itself. It was badly bruised and 'banged up,' but the nerves had not been severed. The CAT scan and MRI had shown no injury to his head or brain, and his cardiovascular system was fine. Now it was time to wait and see how his body would respond and to let him heal some before he began the next steps of the process toward rehabilitation.

The Twins, 1965: Bob (left) and me

Those curls! 1966: Bob (left) and me

The 'belly' pic, Bob (left) and me

Easter with the girls: left to right, left to right, Kathleen, me, Bob and Mary

'Lurch', 1971

Cub Scouts: Bob (left) and me

High School Graduation, 1983: Bob (left) and me

Stevenson Soccer, 1983 MI
State Champs

Family, 1988: Back row, left to right, Kent, me, Dad, Bob, Greg
Front row, left to right, Mary, Mom, Kathleen, Shaun

Me, Dad (center) and Bob (right)

Fun and love: left to right,
Greg, Kathleen, Bob, Mom

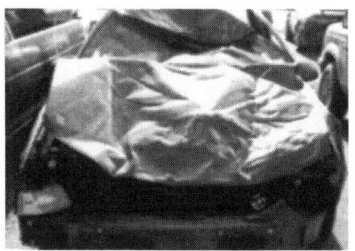

After the impact: March 1995

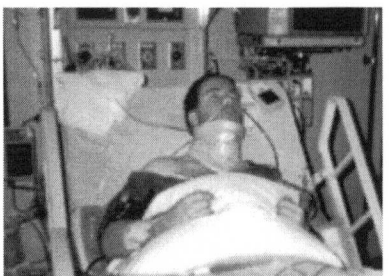

Paralyzed with a C5 spinal cord injury

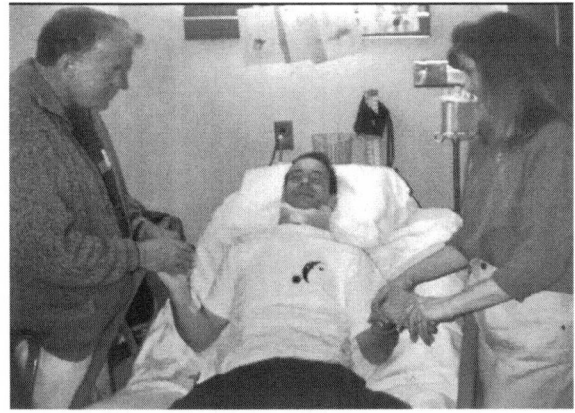

Surrounded in love, Dad and Kathleen working on stimulation techniques

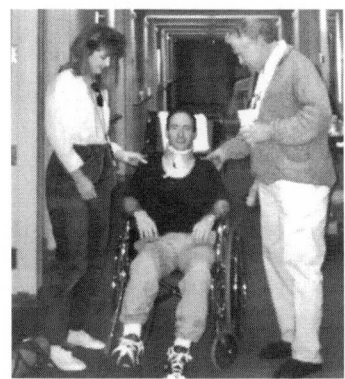

Rolling for a walk with Kathleen and Dad

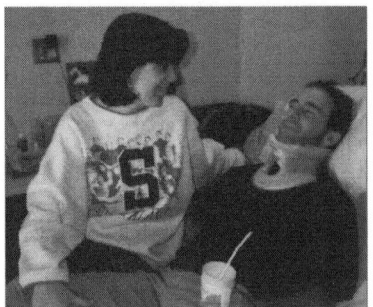

Eyes of love with Shelly

PART TWO
METAMORPHOSIS

SEVEN

THE TRANSFORMATION BEGINS

Now faith is confidence in what we hope for and assur-
ance about what we do not see.

—Hebrews 11:1

The night of my accident was intense, the energy, the faces, the erratic and intense movements from everyone around me, the care and concern complete strangers offered me. I remember being surrounded by nurses and doctors and we were laughing at my jokes when Shelly walked in. I had been continuously asking for her, wondering where she was and why she was not there yet. I was worried about her and how she was doing. Then she walked in, and I felt an enormous sense of relief and gratitude to see her face. I immediately started to relax with the feeling I was going to be alright. It was a whirlwind of activity and people as the medical staff raced to establish my condition and determine the next steps to be taken for my care. Another blessing God gifted to me was the fact that the doctor on call that night for the ER happened to be one of the best neurosurgeons at the time in the United States, Dr. Nelson Macedo. Nash General Hospital, this rural, small-town NC hospital, had two fabulous doctors specializing in neurology assessing me that night. Dr. Rosario Guarino was in attendance as well. They both would also be my surgeons for my upcoming spinal surgery. In the ICU, visiting hours were limited and only for immediate family. Thank goodness they recognized Shelly as immediate family and allowed her full access to me. I saw Shelly as often as they would allow her in to see me. My mom and brother, Bob, flew in by Thursday, and I was so grateful to see them. The sense of relief you feel in a situation of crisis like I was in is immeasurable when someone you love is at your side. My recollection of that time with them is vague and fuzzy, as my spinal surgery was performed on Friday, three days after my accident. They were there for the weekend and their presence brought me a sense of calm and relief. I was grateful Shelly also had some support as well.

I stayed in the ICU for almost two weeks before I was moved to a noncritical-care floor. The transfer from my ICU room to my room a few floors above was a short ride. I was in no shape and a little bit incoherent to really know what was happening, but it was obvious during that time that Shelly's love and compassion for me had set the pace for things to come. I now know how much work and energy was happening behind the scenes. There were phone calls made and emails sent at all hours of the day/night. She was working to keep everyone updated with my condition and progress. This included not only family and friends but also people at work, both from North Carolina and Michigan. Concerned family and friends from hundreds of miles away were all wondering what the next step was going to be. Everything seemed to be happening at a dizzying pace, yet at the same time, it seemed as if time were standing still. I was completely dependent and reliant on others to care for me. This was a first for me, as I was typically used to leading teams and being the person others came to for help. I was vulnerable and had no control of what was happening to me. I quickly discovered how important trust is when your life is in the hands of others. You must believe in those who love you most and know they will take the best care of you. I also realized the importance of having faith in the talent, skill and abilities of those professionals who now were so significant to my future. And most importantly, I relied on my faith in God. He is my Way Maker.

I needed all the strength I could find, and I relied on my positive mindset and sense of humor to play an important part of my recovery. Instead of exhausting myself with negative actions and thoughts, I chose to see goodness in my circumstances. This was my choice to make and one that is a window to my character. My focus sharpened toward my recovery and future. With a long road in front of me, I knew this would not be easy, but my faith was stronger than my fear. I believed God had selected me for this challenge and I ultimately believed if I looked hard enough, there were blessings to be discovered. How I would choose to use these blessings was yet to be determined. Focusing on the positive is not easy, especially during the most trying times in our lives. But it is a choice. We all have choices to make every day of our lives. Even choosing to not do anything is a choice. I believed the success of my future was dependent upon my ability to stay positive. That is hard to do when you cannot move a limb or finger. My thoughts focused on and my mouth spoke to all that I had, not what I had lost. My mentality has always been to look forward and figure out a way to get to the goal in front of me. Use what you have; do what you can.

Being paralyzed created unexpected changes in other aspects of my health and life. One side of my body was hypersensitive, and the other side had little to no sensitivity. My other senses had become much more pronounced and acute. Lights were sharper, footsteps louder, smells more distinct and voices more penetrating. The incessant sounds of hospital equipment and the steps of people walking about became my constant companion of background noise. I could hear footsteps from the hallway and how they became increasingly louder as someone entered the room. I would soon be able to identify who was approaching by the rhythm and heaviness of their footfall and the sounds their shoes made when striking the floor. The slow, methodical steps of my doctor. The fast-moving, light, almost silent steps of my late-night nurse as she raced through her tasks. The heavy, muffled footsteps of a male therapist when he would enter my room for my 'workouts.' The closer someone came to me, the louder the steps resonated in my ears. From my vantage point, lying on my back and not able to move, I was keenly aware of and constantly listening for these different sounds. It was interesting how my sense of hearing became very important to my mental state, thought process and even decision-making. I was surprisingly calm, comfortable and not in much pain. The friendly faces of doctors and nurses were refreshing and offered a sign of hope. Each had a unique job to complete. It is during these moments in life that you learn to swallow your pride. Your level of gratitude becomes limitless and your reliance on others is a strategy in survival. This was still a unique time of discovery for me because it was still being determined how much damage had occurred and how successful the surgery had been. The mission of the spinal fusion had been to add strength, stability and support to the damaged fifth vertebra. Initial feedback shared with my family by my surgeon had been that the surgery was a success. Now it was up to me. To see how my body and my mind would respond. How much usage and return of mobility would occur and how much permanent damage I would have were still unknown. These were questions which would take years to answer. In fact, those changes continue to occur to this day, 26 years later.

In my own room now, outside of the ICU, I worked to settle into what would be my new routine for a while. Shelly had decorated my room with some of my favorite items and sports paraphernalia to inspire me and lift my moods. Of course, she ensured her alma mater, MSU (Michigan State University), was well represented despite the fact (or maybe because of the fact) I was a U of M (University of Michigan) fan. How cruel was that, making me look at all that green and white when I had no control in changing the view? She even dressed me in full MSU gear when I couldn't dress myself and put Sparty in my lap and took pictures! Adding insult to injury, my new store team leader was a Notre Dame graduate. She sent a huge gift box of items to my room, including multiple pieces of Notre Dame gear. As a Michigan fan, how could this possibly get any worse? Of course, it was all in good fun and we had many great laughs over it. Shelly ensured all our favorite Michigan teams, including the Detroit Lions and Tigers, were included in the room decor, plus those from supporting friends. I started receiving hundreds of cards, notes, letters and phone calls from people across the country. These became wallpaper for the room. Positive notes, inspiring messages, pictures, funny cards and more were placed all around so that they were all I could see. With my favorite Detroit Red Wings and Detroit Tigers items on full display, I looked like some kind of pro athlete.

In fact, a nurse walked into my room one day and asked me what team I played for. Talk about an ego boost! I always did want to be a pro. Shelly brought in a boom box so we could listen to our favorite music. Music has always played a significant role in my life, and I would just get lost in it and let the words and messages fill my mind and strengthen my spirit.

So many people reached out to me from all over, including many I had never met. It was incredible, the outpouring of love and support. This poured in not only for me but also for Shelly. We will be eternally grateful for all of those who lifted us up and helped to carry us when we needed it through some of the darkest and scariest times of our lives. The communication tree was in full bloom, with key information being shared from the root of it by Shelly. She did her best to keep others updated, even though she was very much tunnel-focused on me. The hospital staff had placed a recliner chair in the corner of my room, and that became Shelly's bed. She slept in that chair every night while I was in that hospital. If she left, it was only for a few hours because she needed to handle things at home. She never wanted to leave my side, and it made me feel protected and loved. She helped to fill my days with laughter, love, hope, energy and a sense of spirit, which continued my drive to heal. What I was going through, she was going through with me. During those weeks, our relationship deepened in a way which could never be replicated had we not gone through that experience together. It truly made us both realize the gift we had in each other and the depth of our love together.

It may sound like it was all fun and games, but it was far from that. My reality sunk in the day two therapists entered my room for my first workout. *Workout?* Shelly and I looked at each other. How could someone who was paralyzed work out? I was about to find out. I am one of those

92

people who does not like amusement parks. The thought of being on a roller coaster has always made me a little uneasy. Any of those swinging, twirling rides would make me dizzy and sick every time. With that said, I now faced an entirely new way of living. Every time a nurse lifted me, even a slight bit, I felt as if I had just gotten off the Gemini at Cedar Point. My equilibrium was seriously out of whack and the smallest amount of movement sent me spinning. So when these two therapists walked in and said I had a workout coming, I knew I was in trouble. I was nervous about what was to come but ready to tackle whatever it was they were planning to put me through. The therapists approached my bed and got on either side of me. They shared that the plan of the day was to begin getting me to sit up. I thought to myself, *How is this going to work? How do I sit up if I'm paralyzed?* Well, these two were about to show me and assist me in doing just that. They peeled back my blanket and ensured my legs and arms were free and unentangled. I was feeling vulnerable. *Ok*, I thought to myself, *here we go*. One person was at my shoulders and the other near the center of my torso. On a count of three, they began to lift me. I went from lying in a horizontal position to an approximate 35-degree angle. The room immediately began to spin. Dark spots started flashing in my eyes and I began to feel nauseous. Sweat began pouring from my forehead and my body started to shake. They stopped at that angle, held my position for about 10 seconds and then gently lowered me back down to my pillow. I was breathing in fast shallow breaths with sweat pouring off me. Wow! If that small level of movement was that difficult, I had my work cut out for me. Once my heart rate had settled, we did that same exercise one more time before calling it a day. They cheerfully told me to get some rest as they would be seeing me the next day. My new fitness journey had begun! Each morning, my therapists would come into my room, and we would work on this routine, advancing my limits each time. This went on for a few days until it was time for me to graduate to a new challenge. The wheelchair! Get ready, world, it was time for me to roll!

If you have ever experienced a stay in the hospital, you know how quickly modesty becomes obsolete. Imagine being an independent, strong, athletic 30-year-old guy moving toward the height of his career one moment, and in the next, he is lying helplessly in a hospital bed, paralyzed. Paralysis takes the lack of modesty to a whole new level. When you need someone else to care for your every need, you stop being worried about what a nurse or doctor does or does not see. And they will be the first to tell you they have seen it all. I loved those medical professionals who had a sense of humor and continuously used it to help set me at ease during the most difficult and embarrassing of moments. We all need people like that in our lives, those who will keep it real, bring you down to earth and just have fun with those situations you cannot control. So, to that nurse Kathy who walked into my room one day and said to all of us there, "Michael! We gotta wash that hair! You could fry an egg in it!" we still laugh about that today. Thank goodness there are people like Kathy who are willing and capable to do the job they do and are a breath of fresh air while doing it! I know they really appreciated my spirit and my sense of humor as well. A great example of how I helped to make their job a little easier was how I figured out an easier way to take my daily blood-thinner shot. I'm not sure about you, but needles have never been my favorite thing. This became even more of an issue for me after my spinal cord injury. With a spinal cord injury, it is common to have nerve and muscle damage. The types and degree of disability vary greatly depending on the severity of the injury, damage to the cells and which nerve fibers have been impacted. My injury was an incomplete C-5. With an incomplete spinal cord injury, some people may find they have more functioning on one side of the body than the other. This would turn out to be the case for me. I found my body was divided almost literally straight down the middle. The right side of my body is hypersensitive to pain and sensation, and my left side is almost numb to it. Even though I could not move, I did manifest these differences in sensation from the time of my accident. Having to receive a shot in my stomach daily for the blood thinner I needed offered the first opportunity for me to utilize my sensation issues to my benefit. After experiencing the intense pain when the shot was administered on my right side in comparison to the almost nonexistent feeling of it when given on my left side, the choice was clear. This shot was to be given to me only on my left side. Problem solved and no more pain or fear of the needle!

Many hours of my days were spent listening to music. I have always loved music and utilized it to get me through life experiences. I grew up loving the drums, and if you saw me listening to music, you would have seen me tapping my fingers. The beats and rhythms of songs have always been a constant tool to help me process. Now, lying in my bed listening to my favorite songs and musicians, I would imagine I was playing right along with them. In my mind, I was keeping pace with the beat. I felt as if my fingers and toes were tapping and moving to the music. But they weren't. Being paralyzed, that was a surreal experience. It is such a strange sensation for your mind to believe you are making a movement, but that movement is not happening physically. I like to tell people to think of this example: Lay your hand flat on a table and intentionally do not move your fingers, but let your mind take you through the process as if you are tapping your fingers. There is a mind–body connection that is undeniable. Again, do not physically move your fingers, but intently focus on one finger. This sounds strange, but you will feel a twitch in that finger. Just like every movement we make each day, these movements are the result of a strong mind and body connection. Your nerves send signals throughout your body and these signals run continuously up and down your spinal cord, to and from your brain. When the body is subjected to some type of trauma, which damages the cells within the spinal cord or severs the nerve tracts which transmit the signals, disruption to mobility and feeling ensues. Essentially, this amazing highway of information now has roadblocks. Considering my own scenario, I had multiple aspects which have factored into my healing journey, most importantly God. But I too played a very integral role in my own recovery. My positivity and mental state were crucial to my healing. I was doing my own style of mind–body therapy through music and mind-set. What I now know is that I was actually rewiring my brain.

After weeks in the hospital, Shelly and I were in my room alone and we were listening to tunes and talking. Shelly was standing on the right side of my bed. I can't remember what we were talking about, but I remember the music playing in the background and I was experiencing my normal sensation of feeling the beat internally. Suddenly, we saw a slight move-ment of the big toe on my left foot. It was so subtle we almost missed it. Shelly cried, "Did you just move your foot?" We looked at each other in excitement and focused heavily on my feet. I continued to concentrate on the music and felt the pulse of energy in my mind moving through my body. Sure enough, my foot had some movement! We were ecstatic and Shelly went running for the doctor. I had movement! In my feet! This was a HUGE sign of possibility for us. It is interesting how the smallest or seemingly most insignificant examples of progress can have such great meaning. Something others take for granted every day and would not think twice about in a normal instance suddenly becomes critically revealing. All we needed was that one little flicker of hope to know we would not give up on my dream of walking again.

EIGHT

THE POWER OF LOVE

Love never gives up, never loses faith, is always hopeful
and endures through every circumstance.

—*1 Corinthians 13:7*

I feel the need to start this part of my story by sharing the true significance of my journey and recovery. Love. We cannot go through life alone. None of us do it by ourselves. Human beings are meant to be connected, to be part of a larger group or family. We need this sense of community not only during good times or times of celebration but more importantly during times of difficulty. Love includes being there during the worst of times, those times which are most challenging, the ugliest, the hardest. Love can lift you up and pull you out of the darkest days and moments. Love is the power behind hope and believing something greater is ahead. Being present and available for someone during the good times is easy. But this will not sustain a relationship if you are missing the ability to handle the tough stuff. I found my truest relationship when I was not searching for it. It blossomed from a true friendship into something so much greater than I could have ever imagined. When God created Adam, despite Adam's greatness, God knew Adam needed a companion to complement him and help him along his way. The companion God planned for me is Shelly.

You will discover through this story that this is not only my own. It is so much more. You will discover a common theme of Shelly's unending strength and love for me—her countless hours spent sleeping in a chair, exhausted by her emotions and the many responsibilities she was carrying. She was my link to my family, our friends and our Target family. She is strong, fearless and a precious gift my Creator blessed me with. This was not the first time I witnessed the depth of her love, yet it has been one consistent strength in our relationship. The story of Shelly is one of compassion, her fierce love for me and being true to what she believes in. Shelly has been by my side, in sickness and in health. She has been my rock, and her love and energy established the foundation for my recovery. She has my heart.

My family has been equally significant in my life and recovery after the accident. Not only did my mom and Bob come to my side in those first crucial days and through my surgery, but the other half of my family was also ready to come next. My sisters, Mary and Kathleen, dad and Kathleen's husband, Greg, were on the way. They loaded themselves into Mary's van and left Ann Arbor, destined for North Carolina. On a mission, they drove straight through. Not knowing what to expect upon arrival at the hospital, they all entered my room with my dad leading the way. He stepped up to my bed and immediately grabbed my hand and gave it a strong squeeze with love in his eyes. I was so glad to see them all and felt a huge sense of relief, comfort and love to have them there. It was almost overwhelming the amount of emotion which overtook me. Talking to my dad first, Mary and Kathleen took a quick moment to step back out into the hallway. Their first sight of me lying in that hospital bed was shocking to them. Nothing they had done prepared them for what they saw. To say I was not looking my best was an understatement. I had already lost a considerable amount of weight. I was wearing a Philadelphia collar to stabilize my neck, sporting a sexy hospital gown, was unshaven, had wild, uncombed hair and was basically unmoving. Upon seeing me they both needed to gain some composure. I would not know this happened until years later. After shedding a few tears, they quickly returned to the room so they could get to my side. This first interaction with them was important to me. I put on my best face and pretended I was feeling good. I could only move my head and neck, but my mind and spirit were the same. Seeing my smile and my sense of humor still intact immediately set them at ease. Having Greg be there with them was icing on the cake. It felt like 'home' as they all surrounded me, and we got to talking. I could see Shelly was so happy to see them all too. Hugs, smiles and laughter filled the room. We had to be the loudest room on the floor, and we did not care. I was so grateful they had made it to North Carolina safely and we were just happy to all be together. I noticed something in Kathleen's arms and asked her about it. She was carrying a cow cookie jar and walked over to set it on the counter near my bed. "Please tell me that thing is loaded with your famous cookies (my favorite: oatmeal raisin and chocolate chip)," I said to her. She smiled and opened the lid. "Mooooo...," came the noise. What?! The thing was actually mooing. We all bursted out laughing and this was the immediate icebreaker and mood lifter we all needed. And yes, filled to the rim were my favorite cookies made with her love.

Their visit was special in so many ways and I was amazed at how strong everyone was. They gave me additional strength and purpose to recover. I am sure everyone was uncomfortable. It is hard to imagine what to say in a situation when you see a loved one whom you have known one way and now, they are paralyzed, yet acting as if everything was going to be ok. Did we know this to be true? No, no one did. But we all believed it to be true because I did. So, our truth was our reality. My humor, mindset and spirit showcased I was still me. It made everyone realize I was the same person inside even though I was broken on the outside. We joked and laughed at the stories we were sharing. To have them talk with me, joke and share as we always have made me feel 'normal.' Despite the difficulty of my situation, our love for one another and our relationships were not compromised. In fact, I believe they were strengthened. Facing tough situations, people have two options, lean in or run. Thankfully, my family and most of those who surrounded me chose the first option. We would get through this together and our love would give us the power to do it.

Each person in my family had their own unique gifts and abilities to give me support. But a spinal cord injury is frightening and difficult for all as recovery is so uncertain. What was amazing to me was the strength I experienced from those who loved me. Their sheer presence is what I needed most. A fond memory I have is being surrounded by my family. It makes us all laugh every time we think of it. Greg had grabbed one hand and Kathleen the other. My dad had a foot and Mary took hold of the other foot (even though she said she drew the line in the sand massaging my bunions and corns). To be surrounded like this by my family, each one holding a part of me and massaging my limbs as they talked and laughed, was just pure love. With me diagnosed with weakness of all four limbs, they literally had their hands full. I am sure this felt very unusual for everyone, but even when my sensitivity on both sides was limited and my muscles were not moving, the power of touch was bringing healing to my body. Those simple acts of kindness made a big difference. This gave everyone something to do during a time when they felt so helpless. I loved all the attention as they worked to help me heal. A feeling of love and hope was present throughout the room. I remember meeting a woman years later during an event Shelly and I were a part of. In sharing our stories with each other, she talked about when she had had a severe accident and was in the hospital. She shared one thing which had a profound impact on her while she was in the hospital. For her, people had been afraid to touch her because she looked so fragile. At a time when she needed that physical connection with others most, it had been missing. All she wanted was a hug from those she loved. But because she had injured her back, her loved ones were afraid they could do her more harm by mistake if they moved her the wrong way. Once she was released from the hospital and was deep into her recovery, she remembered this profound impact on her psyche while she was in such a vulnerable state. It had made such an impact on her that she decided to start a nonprofit for hospitals to offer the power of hugs and touch to people who needed it most. Her story made me remember my own poignant moment of my family surrounding me and giving me the greatest gift of love.

Another funny experience was my mealtime. My meals were delivered to my room. The expectation from the hospital staff was for me to start working on my independence and feeding myself was part of that agenda. That was a good plan. For when I actually started to regain some movement in my arms and hands. But during the time when my family was visiting, I was not quite there yet. So here again, everyone played a role. When my meal was delivered, each person was responsible for a portion of my meal. They surrounded my bed and got ready for action. I so wish we had this moment on video because it would be hysterical! Mary had the spoon, Kathleen the fork, Shelly had my beverage with a straw, Greg was ready with the cookie for dessert and Dad was the supervisor of the project. "Are you ready?" Shelly asked. "Let's go," I said. We all started laughing and then it started. "Fork!" I called out. Kathleen moved to my mouth with the food on the fork. They all stared at me as I chewed and swallowed. "Spoon!" I called next. Mary was right there, not spilling a drop. "Sip!" came next. And on it went. We all started laughing as it became a contest of who could do the best job with their assigned tool. Until we were all talking and laughing and I started choking. 'Sip, sip, sip!' I was trying to choke out. But Shelly came to the rescue as she raced to my mouth with my drink and straw. What a trip to be fed that way! It sure was one of the most unique meals I have ever had in my life. Your family has to really love you to share in such a personal and intimate way something which is so basic and elemental for most. By doing this for me, they helped to make me feel as normal as I possibly could have felt during that awkward and uncertain time.

While my family was visiting, we had many deep and meaningful conversations. We shared with my sisters how challenging it had been for us going through this traumatic event and how especially hard it was because Shelly and I were not yet married. They both knew our intentions all along had been to get married after we had settled into the area. Mary reminded me of a conversation we had prior to leaving Michigan. She had advised me that before we finalized plans to move to North Carolina, I needed to make sure Shelly was 'the one' prior to making a big move across the country. She and I both had no idea how crucial that great advice would come to be. Not only was Shelly 'the one' but now she was also put in a position to make important and potentially life-altering decisions for us both. As we all visited one early afternoon, Shelly had to go back to Raleigh to handle some things. While she was gone, my sisters and I further discussed our plans for the future and my intentions to propose to her. This was more important to me now than ever. We all talked in detail and I thought to myself, *What if I had a ring? What if the current situation were different? Where would we be?* Almost instantaneously, my sisters had ideas and started talking. At first, they both offered up their own wedding rings as a temporary option until I could get a real ring for Shelly and propose properly on my own two feet. Then Kathleen realized she was wearing my grandmother's ring, which she had recently gotten resized and additional diamonds added to. She offered me this ring to use, and then Shelly could wear it as long as needed until I could pick one out for her myself. It was perfect! We hatched a plan for me to propose in the hospital. I wanted to do it while my family was still visiting so they could share in the celebration with us. I wanted Shelly to know my entire family was proposing to her, not just me. Mary and Kathy went down to the gift shop to see if they could find a good prop for me to use. There sat a round plastic container with candy in it. This would do! They opened it up and tied the ring to a piece of candy in the center of the bowl. They rewrapped the candy container with a beautiful bow on top and had it ready for me, on the table near my bed. We shared the plan with the nursing staff, and they too were excited. I couldn't wait for Shelly to return from Raleigh. My family left before she was due back to ensure that we had some time together alone. I was super excited but nervous at the same time. Both of my sisters had given me confidence that Shelly would say yes. They had shared how they knew we were in love before we even left Michigan, but now they had been witnessing the love Shelly had for me which was on another level. The power of love between us was palpable. The honesty of my sisters and that conversation had given me the courage I needed. The nurses helped me set the stage in my room. They adjusted the lighting as best they could and lit some candles. They had the right music ready with Michael Bolton playing in the background. Now I was ready and just needed Shelly to return. The only thing undetermined was *will she say 'yes'?* I think you know the answer to that question by now.

Moments in our lives—they happen countless times every day to every one of us. The question is, do we see the significance of these moments when they are happening? Do we recognize and seize the moment for the greatness it can offer our lives? Tomorrow is not guaranteed for any of us. Yesterday has already happened. What you have is right here, right now. What are you going to do with this moment? To experience the full power of love life has to offer. Whatever you do, don't miss it.

The power of love should be visible not only during trials; it is always around you. You not only feel it; love speaks to you. It whispers into your thoughts and flows into your heart when you least expect it. A great example of this from our life is one day Shelly took a call from her dad. He was calling to ask if we wanted to take a trip back to Europe with her parents later that year. We had gone once before and had had a fabulous time. Now they were planning another trip and wanted us to go again. Shelly told him we would love to, but we could not really afford it at that time. Plus, we were crazy busy with work. She hung up and shared the conversation with me. As we talked, I said, "Shelly, we need to think about this. We had so much fun with your parents last time. It was an incredible trip. And now they are going back and to so many other countries. It could be a trip of a lifetime. Your parents are getting older, and your dad has had health issues. You never know if we will have this opportunity again." We talked more in depth about it and decided we needed to just go. God whispered into our hearts, 'Don't miss the moment.' So, Shelly called her dad back and told him we would love to go. We were going to figure out a way to make it happen, but we definitely wanted to take this trip with them. It truly was the trip of a lifetime, almost worthy of its own book. So many precious moments and priceless memories we have are from that trip. And it was the last one we would ever take again with Shelly's parents all together. Her dad passed away later that year due to a massive heart attack. Gone in an instant. The message here is don't miss the moments. There is nothing more powerful than the power of love. It can sustain you through all situations, the good and the bad.

NINE

RED TEAM

Surely you have granted him unending blessings and
made him glad with the joy of your presence.

—Psalms 21:6

Surrounding yourself with great people is a key to success in life. We all have strengths and weaknesses. Having people around you who help to balance your own is key. Sometimes we have the ability to select people for our circle, and other times, God places the right people in our path for a reason. It is important to recognize not only the gifts others can provide to you in your life but also what you can provide to others.

It was a quiet afternoon, and I was lying in my bed doing one thing which took me back in time and made me feel like me. With 70s' and 80s' rock 'n' roll music playing at my bedside, I was unknowingly trying to make a mind–body connection in rewiring my brain. In my mind I was tapping to the music, although my fingers and feet were still not moving. The rumor was that I would be moving on to a rehab facility soon, destination unknown. I was making good progress and moving closer to the next phase of my recovery. The goal at Nash General Hospital was to provide the critical care necessary after my accident and to stabilize my injury. This of course did involve some surgeries and the initial stages of rehabilitation. Stabilization means the life-altering aspects have passed and you are now ready for further physical rehabilitation. This goal had been achieved. The next step for me now was to see how much return of movement and sensation was possible for me.

I was eager to move forward. Progress is progress, and any amount of that I experienced provided hope and was the motivation I needed to push for the next goal. About a week after my surgery, two unfamiliar people, a man and a woman, walked into my room. They introduced themselves and said, "Hello, Michael, we are from Wake Medical." Instantly, I became aware and alert and wondered why they had travelled to see me. They both were very professionally dressed and they politely asked if they could sit down to have a conversation with me. Because it was very common for visitors to come into my room, even after visiting hours, I felt comfortable. I knew they were there for a reason, and I was anxious to hear what they had to say. Rehab and physical therapy services at Wake Medical are designed to connect a smooth continuum of care for children, adults and their families. Wake Medical Rehabilitation has a stellar reputation for the care and services they provide. What I did not realize was having the opportunity to be part of their program was not a guarantee. They have a discriminating process in determining who they believe will be successful in their program. At the hardest and most traumatic point in my life, I would never have believed I would have to interview as a potential new patient in order to be accepted in. This medical facility which admits thousands of spinal cord, brain injury and stroke victims every year was now interviewing me to determine if I had the right mindset for their program. With careful, professionally crafted questions, they were working to determine if I had what it took to successfully complete their program and if they could offer me what I needed. Their questions covered most of my life, from the present day going back into my childhood. I remember thinking this was the most detailed and personally invasive interview I had ever gone through. I also thought to myself, *What if I don't do well?* We had a long but what I thought was a good conversation. They said their goodbyes and said they would be in touch with me soon. Shelly and I were both encouraged, and I remember sleeping very well that night.

The next morning, the lights came on early. I was awoken with a sense of urgency. There were two new and unfamiliar attendees at my bedside. They had news for me and were ready to transfer me onto a gurney. I was being discharged from Nash General and preparing to travel back to Raleigh. It appeared I had passed the interview with flying colors and I was on my way to the Wake Medical Rehabilitation Hospital. My limo (a.k.a. ambulance) was waiting outside to escort me there in dramatic fashion. The hour-long ride would be a grueling and uncomfortable commute to my soon-to-be home for the next few months. Shelly would gather my belongings and follow behind to join me in my new home away from home. She was excited, as this would be much closer to home. It would be so much easier for her to juggle her time between visiting me, returning to work and handling things for us at home. This ambulance ride would be a very different experience than the one I had just had a month before. Here

I was, once again staring at the bright lights in an ambulance, but now I was having a friendly and relaxed conversation with the EMTs. I ensured to thank them for all the care they provided to people during their work-day, especially for me. When I arrived at Wake Medical, I remember going through a brief meeting as part of the admissions process before being brought to the room I would occupy for the next two to three months. The rest of the day was spent ensuring I was comfortable and being attended to and meeting many everyday heroes. Nurses, doctors and administrative assistants came and went, handling their daily routine with excellence. Even though I had a good experience and was treated well at Nash General, Wake Medical felt different. There was a different vibe and energy in the air, and everyone appeared to be so happy to be there. Maybe it was just my impression, but I felt at home almost immediately. After the ambulance ride, I was exhausted and needed some well-deserved rest. I was eager to get started the following day on the next leg of my journey. I was not sure exactly what was ahead, but I did know I would need some good, solid rest in order to handle it. Now it was time for me to live up to the positive reputation I had developed over the years. It was time to get busy. As I drifted off to sleep, I felt calm and settled.

When I awoke the next morning, my bed was surrounded by a group of people. A tall, abrasive woman spoke for the group and said, "Hello, Michael! We are the Red Team. We are here to get you back on your feet." Wow! I had an entire team dedicated just to me? Instantly I felt very special. Everyone looked very professional and eager to get started. On my team I had a clinical case manager (CCM), a physical therapist (PT), an occupational therapist (OT), a therapeutic recreation specialist and a rehab neuropsychologist. The CCM held the role of team leader and was the liaison between me, my family and medical team. This medical team was a group of highly trained professionals reporting directly to the rehabilitation physicians and physician assistants (PAs). It was very clear from the onset that I was in good hands. These would become people I would be forever grateful to. The tall, commanding woman was identified as Debby, my PT. She was exceptionally professional. Not only was she effective, strong, detailed and caring but she was also a powerlifter in her spare time. I never saw her without a smile and I looked forward to seeing her every day. We had an instantaneous bond. She was good at pretending to like my jokes and did her best to appear interested in my many shoplifter stories. Debby was never in a bad mood and she treated me like I was a part of her family. An obvious leader and mentor, other PTs would shadow her for training and development in their own positions. She set high standards and expectations. She expected people to give their best effort in whatever it was they were doing. She worked hard and was fully committed to her task at hand, and she expected others to do the same. This expectation was for both patients and those she worked alongside. She was a true professional and a great person.

In physical contrast to Debby, Darlene, my OT, was a very petite, muscle-bound young woman. She also demonstrated great strength in personality and performance and instantly made me feel like we had been friends for years. Darlene was a bodybuilder who had once been featured in *Muscle* & Fitness magazine. Her smile and energy brought hope to my early morning routine. Darlene was tough and instantly felt like a sister. She was smart, fun and extremely professional. She was the first person I saw every day, and she made it very clear that I was going to work hard on her watch. Like a drill sergeant, Darlene didn't mess around. I was blessed to have such an experienced, professional team and was excited to get started. A therapy schedule was created with daily, clear objectives and goals. The first week was crucial in determining exactly what my treatment program, goals for rehab, discharge plans and anticipated length of stay would be. Each day, there was a detailed conference report reviewed in depth with me and Shelly and signed off by the lead physicians. My main objective was to become 'independent.' Independence Day was a big day at Wake Medical. It was the main event in rehab, and for someone with my type of injury, this would be a monumental achievement.

I was grateful to be at Wake Rehab. I often wondered how many people did not make it through the interview process and were turned down for their program. Where are they today and how are they doing with their injuries or illnesses? I am confident that my positive mindset played an important role in my entire recovery, but that initial interview set the course for things to come. I truly believe my faith, spirit and mindset are the driving reasons I am walking today. Second of course to the will of God. Shelly and I had prayed I would be able to attend a rehab program closer to home in Raleigh. There were some very good rehabilitation hospitals across the region that were recommended, but an out-of-state recovery program was not part of our plan if we could avoid it. Being in a facility in our city and not a far drive from our home was a blessing. Now it was time for me to focus. I knew that every great team is only as good as the weakest link. It was very important for me to remember that a spinal cord injury is life altering. A spinal cord injury patient does not lose the ability to feel emotion, learn, work, play or live life to the fullest possible. They may just have to do it differently. Learning to adapt is not an option. How you do it is your option. Being surrounded by great people is a critical component to help someone be successful through this process. I knew this Red Team, this group of people dedicated and committed to my recovery and future, was an incredible gift and blessing. And I was not about to waste it. I was ready and I had recovery on my mind.

That first day at Wake Rehab, Shelly took advantage of the time I was out of my room. She moved in and decorated my room with many of the cards and letters we brought from the hospital. She also added some new and extra elements. She thought she was quite funny when I returned from my day's activities to find my room shining with cow lights strung all throughout the room along with lots of other cow-themed decor. Front and center was my now favorite cookie jar—the mooing cow. Everyone, including me, thought this was funny and extra special. It was a clever way of making my room away from home feel like 'me' and would bring a smile to anyone and everyone who entered the room. Shelly had no idea what she started with the whole cow theme. This was just the beginning.

TEN

NO TIME FOR TALK

Let us not become weary in doing good, for at the proper
time we will reap a harvest if we do not give up.

—Galatians 6:9

There she was, standing at my door with a huge smile on her face.
It was Darlene, accompanied by another occupational therapist. They
walked in pushing a wheelchair and asked if I was ready to get started. I
was already awake after a sleepless night. I was still getting used to a new
room, a roommate and nervousness about what lay ahead. It was hard to
sleep. It was day one, the first day of the rest of my life. Darlene asked what I
wanted to wear and started rummaging through my personal things. After
she selected my socks, underwear, shirt and sweatpants, she reached down,
grabbed my shoes and threw them in my lap. Knowing I had very limited
use of my limbs, she said, "Go ahead, put those on." *Are you kidding me!* I

thought? But she looked serious. "I am not going to do it for you," she said and gave me a couple of minutes to think about my next move. Knowing I did not have one, she said she would help on this first day, but if I wanted to get dressed in the future, I would have to do it myself. She was not fooling around. She was making it clear she was not there to do it for me. She was going to assist moderately as needed, but it was up to me to dress myself. As I prepared myself for this new challenge, I knew one thing, I was not going to be putting on my own socks and shoes any time soon. Darlene went on to explain the rules of engagement on her watch. She pulled out a small placard covered in plastic and attached it to my new wheels. She explained that the goal was to become independent in each area on the card. As each goal was met, I would receive a green sticker to place next to that category. This would signify my progress. I knew this was not going to happen overnight, but it would be a good visual and I was motivated and willing to put in the work. They may have been considered 'The Red Team,' but all I wanted to see was green!

As I said before, there is no room for modesty in rehab or the hospital. I was dependent on everyone around me and I felt the pressure to be a good patient. Initially I would need maximum assistance with grooming and eating, and I was still on an aggressive bowel and bladder program. One top goal was to be removed from a catheter and be able to use the toilet without assistance. This is the most basic of human functions and most people don't even think about it until your 'plumbing' no longer works properly. Then it becomes a pretty big deal. To me, this seemed like a good first goal to achieve. After all, most of us do not want a party in the bathroom every time you have to 'go.' It is one of those basic human functions I think we all want to do privately. It is not a lot of fun having people standing next to you while you are trying to make things happen. Nope, I did not want to have the need for assistance on this one. This was a top priority to achieve independence for sure!

Every morning was filled with routines. Selecting an outfit to impress the other patients, proper grooming and putting on my best game face were key priorities. Each morning Darlene arrived to take me through the steps. After my clothes were selected, my shoes and socks would be thrown in my lap and the day would begin. I discovered that being transferred from my bed to a chair would continue to present those familiar head rushes that I experienced in Nash General. I had come a long way to tolerate this type of movement, but it was still a struggle through dizziness. On the days I was allowed to shower, I was rolled into a shower stall and given assistance to get a thorough cleansing. Those were magical moments compared to the sponge baths given at Nash General. I quickly understood the true meaning of gratitude for the most basic of human needs in life. The first time in the shower was a little nerve-wracking. Something which had always been so private was now a team effort. Thank goodness Darlene had a great sense of humor, because without it, this process would have been even more uncomfortable. She had an extra special tool—the infamous yellow scrub glove I needed to wear for each shower. There is a first for everything. It looked like Michael Jackson's white glove, only it was yellow. Like his sparkles and glitter, my yellow glove had extra rivets to get the job done and was not necessarily designed for comfort. I guess the rivets did glisten a bit from the water. On one side of my body, I could barely feel the rivets. On the other side, it was pure torture. Darlene said it was to be a regular part of my routine, so if I wanted to be clean, I needed to endure the rivets. I would have done anything for that hot water and to feel completely clean. Something so simple to most became therapeutic and pure heaven to me. After my showers and awkward attempts to put on my socks and shoes, it was time to get to work. Getting dressed was only the beginning of my therapy sessions for the day.

Rolling down the hall each morning, I would pass the nurses' station across from the elevator. Most mornings, I was greeted with a cheery voice saying to me, "Hello, Michael! Have a beautiful day." I could only see the top of her head from the seat of my chair and I found out this woman's name was June. It made me feel very special that she knew my name and to be greeted in such a friendly way each day. It was like the show *Cheers*, where everyone knows your name. I looked forward to this daily pump up on my way down to the therapy room. My days were very routine yet filled with different experiences. Each session began with transfers from my chair to a mat. The mat is where the magic would happen. Starting with maximum assistance, the goal was to progress to moderate assistance, and then hopefully I would be doing the transfer on my own. One could only dream. With a team of therapists working with me each day, the days were grueling and an eye-opener as to the extent of my injury. Basic movements would be accompanied by moderate to maximum assistance. Arms, legs, hands and feet were always being moved by others. My level of muscle strength and range of motion were now being evaluated and addressed with intensity. I was starting over like a child. Filled with gratitude for the smallest improvement, my confidence was reinforced with a smile or a congratulatory response from my therapist. We worked hard with all the various pieces of equipment available to assist in my therapies. The end goal was our continual focus to improve, stay motivated and transition into a life that would be perceived as somewhat normal. 'Normal' is a very relative term though, isn't it? What exactly does that even mean? And I surely was anything but typical or what others might consider to be 'normal.' So my focus was showing improvement every day. As long as we were moving forward, I knew I was on the right path. The progress would be gradual, but the direction was clear.

I worked hard every day and was encouraged by other patients also struggling through their own adverse situations. The therapy room was a bridge to independence filled with inspiring people, each with their own scenario of illness or injury. I made progress from moving from a seated position to a standing one. Then I advanced from the ability to just stand to being able to take a few careful steps with assistance. Then came the ability to move a few feet independently with the assistance of a handrail. This seems so insignificant to most, but it was very exciting for me with each monumental achievement. Slowly I became stronger and soon I had progressed with my stool pivots. Stool pivots are the action of moving from a seated or stool position to a standing position. I was now transferring from a seated position to a standing position with limited assistance. Then it was time. The moment had come to see how many steps I could take independently, without any support. I was up for the challenge, but a bit nervous. All eyes were on me as I tried to take a short journey. I was only able to make it a few steps, but when I did, the floodgates opened. I remember trying to hold back my tears, but as they came pouring down my face, the other patients in the immediate area began to cheer me on. It was overwhelming to have complete strangers who were battling their own challenges now motivating me to take another step. The power of humanity and grace is awesome. We cannot lose sight of the significance engaging and encouraging others can have on inspiring and helping them to achieve greater things in their own journey.

My time at rehab was precious and the clock was ticking. I knew the significance of every moment I had with my therapists in shaping my future. One day I found myself being escorted through the rehabilitation room and down a hallway into an office area. I had this strange feeling like I was on my way to the principal's office. Maybe it was because I was making great progress that day and still had adrenaline flowing through my veins from the day's grueling workout that I felt disrupted in my agenda for the day. Or maybe I just did not want to slow my momentum. I truly just wanted to keep moving, to keep striving toward my goal of being able to walk again. Or at least in my case, my version of it. We approached a room, a door swung open, and we were invited in. As I wheeled in and sat in my wheelchair, I was asked by a doctor if I had time to chat. Thinking to myself, *Not really, I need to get back to work*, the neuropsychologist started talking without waiting for my answer. "Hello, Michael, how are you doing? How do you feel about yourself right now?" Instantly I thought that was a weird question. Of course I was doing fine! My progress reports and verbal feedback from my team were all good. So why was I being asked how I was I doing? I knew deep down inside that the neuropsychologist was just doing his job and wanted to learn a little more about me and wanted to help, but I felt a burning desire to get back to therapy. He began our session, asking me various questions, trying to unlock my inner thoughts. His questions were designed to pull emotion from me. He was wanting to pull out the negative emotions I may have had tied to my accident and injury, to my current state of health and the life changes I was experiencing. This was a very different style of therapy than I had become accustomed to, and one which I did not appreciate. I tried to explain that I was not angry, sad or disappointed because of my accident. He felt I was living in denial and was not properly coming to terms with the reality of my situation and what life ahead could hold for me. He pressed on and explained that our conversation was an attempt to evaluate me to see where additional therapies would be needed and to help facilitate discharge plans. To prepare me for the real world when I would leave the hospital. He believed as much as I was improving, I would be confined to the use of a wheelchair for the rest of my life. He also believed I did not have a sense of reality and therefore I was not preparing at all for this possibility to be my future. Respectfully, I knew he was trying to help, but my priority was to make continuous progress with the ultimate goal of becoming independent. My priority was to return to the person I used to be, and if that was not possible, to become a new version of myself. Bigger, better and stronger. I felt like he was wasting my time and precious opportunities to focus on healing my body. In my mind and in my world, there was no time to talk. I especially did not have time to talk to someone with the mindset of this doctor. Not for *my* future. I was ready to get back to work and see where my new normal could take me. The only way to do this was through the blood, sweat and tears in the therapy room. As soon as I could, I communicated with my case manager and shared that I felt that these 'conversations with a purpose' with the neuropsychologist were not necessary for me and they were distracting me from what was most important in my scenario. I wanted to discontinue them. My message was heard. These meetings were discontinued for me.

The rehabilitation process highlighted a new reality for me—spasticity. Spasticity is often associated with paralysis and muscle weakness. Clinically, spasticity results from the loss of inhibition of motor neurons, causing excessive velocity-dependent muscle contractions. In other words, violent spasms in your muscles which you have no control over. It was explained to me in simple terms. Think of how your body reacts when you wake up in the morning. You might be familiar with the 'cat stretch.' You know the stretch, when you wake up you extend your arms in the air and gently stretch them out with a big yawn. You work to stretch your legs as you move to stand. This stretching process is sending signals through your body via your spinal cord letting your body know you are ready and preparing to get moving and tackle the day. When spinal trauma occurs, this normal messaging is now interrupted. The proper messages are now disrupted and may not make it to the location of injury. This can cause violent spasms. I was told this would be a regular part of my new normal and I was given medication in an attempt to minimize them. If you saw my right leg fly up in the direction of the ceiling every morning, you would have probably thought I was being electrocuted. But I quickly discovered as bad as they were, they could be used to strengthen surrounding muscles. That's right. I could use this painful, alarming muscle surprise to my advantage. Sometimes, when at the worst, it felt like my leg was being ripped out of socket. Other times it was an involuntary movement that reminded me that my body was still alive and crying out to me to keep moving. Do not give up. It showcased to me my body was still alive and struggling to heal itself and was signaling to me it was becoming stronger through the pain of those spastic movements.

With slow and steady progress, I was eager and hungry for improvement. With every small step, big or small muscle twitch or new sensation, I felt like I was on a path to my goal of independence. I was striving to earn those green dots on my placard. Seeing the green was my visual motivation showcasing the improvement from one day to the next. It was a similar concept to how I tracked theft and fraud in my job. Visualization is a key tool to help people reach desired objectives. It is a great way to assess your current status and to more clearly see obstacles standing in the way of reaching your goals. It helps me to problem-solve and troubleshoot through obstacles. And of course, Shelly's mantra of "Go Green!" now had a more important usage than just cheering for her beloved Spartans.

My long-term goals were still a long way out, but I could feel my body coming back to life through every activity. My muscles had atrophied significantly and quickly after my accident during those first weeks of inactivity. It is shocking to see how quickly a body can change in such a short period of time. Our focus on rebuilding muscle memory and strength was paying off more quickly for my larger muscle groups. It was much more difficult to activate those smaller muscles and more fine tendons and arteries serving them. I was told that these delicate muscles are the last to return to normal functioning after a spinal cord injury, if they return at all. I soon realized that some of the simplest everyday tasks relied on these delicate muscles and tendons to work properly. This was Darlene's focus. One priority was to strengthen my grip and improve the dexterity of my fingers and hands. Darlene had unique exercise techniques to focus on fine muscles and motor skills. The first one was a fun one. We started with the game of Jenga. My first goal was to remove five blocks from the tower and place them on the table without knocking the entire tower over. Challenge accepted! My newest goal became being the rehab champion at Jenga! Simple goal I know, but one does need to have goals which show some progress, right? Another activity example like Jenga was the coin exercise. This was a bit harder for me. Darlene would put a variety of coins flat on a table. These coins consisted of pennies, nickels, dimes and quarters. My challenge was to be able to pick up each of these by category and stack them in rows. It was very interesting to recognize the difficulty of this when your fingers do not move well. We started with quarters, the thickest of the coins. A struggle at first, this exercise helped to get those nerves activated and to focus on those small, delicate muscles. It took me multiple sessions until I was able to pick up the dimes off the table and stack them without knocking over my newly stacked columns.

My left hand, along with my entire left side, was returning faster than my right side. The sensations of hot and cold, along with pain, were also progressing at different paces and levels. These were being carefully monitored by my team. I felt Darlene saw this as a good opportunity to torture me with one of her fancy electronic devices. She hooked up a strange device with wires attached to my fingers. Interesting. This device was an electrical stimulation called an E-stim. An E-stim is commonly used by OTs to use mild electrical pulses through the skin to awaken injured muscles and to manipulate nerves. At first it was easy. Darlene started with a low intensity on each finger/digit, asking continuously what I was feeling as she slowly turned up the volume. She was working to assess my sensation levels and pain tolerance. She would ask, "Can you feel this?" Depending on my response, she would gradually increase the level of stimulation. It was so weird to watch my fingers, hands and arms respond. And Darlene didn't hold back. When I said I could tolerate a certain number, usually at a low level, she would smile, spin the dial on the intensity meter and crank it up. I swear this was her favorite tool in therapy. She was having way too much fun, smiling through the entire process as she watched me and my body react to the stimulus. As my fingers were being manipulated and acting of their own accord to the shock, I was also having fun knowing that I was making progress. I'll never forget this contraption, and I was weirdly grateful for the long hours of torture with it. I am sure Darlene had a blast while her laughter and bright smile painted the picture for her thoughts.

As time progressed through rehab, I made my rounds and worked with every member of my team. I felt like the plans were covering every aspect of my rehabilitation and I was still amazed at how everyone was enthusiastic and excited and anticipated every step of my progress. I was like a big experiment. With every improvement there were celebrations. When I struggled, we course-corrected. One day, I was brave enough to ask my recreational therapist if we could incorporate a soccer ball into my recovery. She eagerly agreed and we got down to business. Knowing that my skills would be a far cry from my high school and college soccer days, we started out slow. We started from the beginning with the basics as if I were a child. I did what I could. With moderate assistance, I transferred from my wheelchair down to a mat and onto the floor to a seated position. My legs were stretched out in front of me. She placed the ball on the ground, and with assistance, I moved my leg and placed my foot on top of the ball. At that moment, the significance of visualization became more powerful than I had ever realized. There is nothing really exciting about someone sitting on the floor with a leg extended and their foot resting on a soccer ball. The exercise room surely did not smell like freshly cut grass. And the crowd surrounding me was nothing like that crowd I had experienced in 1982 as we won the State Championship game at the Flint Atwood Stadium. But there I sat, once again staring at a soccer ball and gently moving it from side to side, attempting to not let it roll away from me. I was able to drown out the noise of the other patients in the therapy room and I began to visualize the game I once loved. The ball became my focus and a source of strength. In my mind I felt like a defender again. This became one of my favorite parts of my therapy, as it allowed me to be me. Each time I worked with my RT, I looked forward to 'getting back on the field.' Each session I became stronger and brought progress and hope. New goals were created using the soccer ball, similar to what I had experienced during my days of training as a soccer player. One progress report showcased the results I was achieving but also illustrated how much further I had yet to go:

Patient will demonstrate the ability to hold a soccer ball between his feet elevated at least 3 inches from the ground for at least 35 seconds during a 30-minute treatment session.

This was not an achievement for an able-bodied athlete to be proud of, but it was big for me. Working with the soccer ball helped me to dig deeper into my subconscious and visualize being back on the field. This was empowering as I progressed in strength and ability. Soccer ball training continued through the entirety of my stay at Wake Rehab. Of course, additional exercises were added, which were designed to set me up for the real world once I was released and returned home. I progressed to maneuvering stairs, being able to climb two or three steps in a session with assistance. This helped to strengthen my balance and gain confidence along the way. I was also offered the option of doing water therapy. I was very hesitant to do this. I had never been a good swimmer, unlike Shelly, who had been swimming since she was 4. Because of my injuries and limitations, I was terrified of going into the water. That quickly changed once I decided to try it. Protected by life vests and floating devices, I was slowly lifted from my wheelchair and lowered into the water. With therapists surrounding me, I felt safe and ready to try the experience. Once I was in the water,

I felt alive! As I floated, the water helped me to move my arms and legs. This was a wonderful sensation as I moved my limbs and torso so much easier and more fluidly than when on dry land. I stayed in the water until I was exhausted. It was exhilarating and I couldn't wait to do it again. Along with using the soccer ball, water therapy became a new favorite activity for me. And it turned out to be very significant in helping to strengthen my muscles and motor skills in a safe and less demanding way on my body. It made me feel alive, like an athlete, and helped me to visualize a greater future ahead.

ELEVEN

THE DAY I LOST MY WHEELS

Whether you turn to the right or to the left, your ears will
hear a voice behind you saying,
"This is the way, walk in it."

—Isaiah 30:21

What do you see? Literally, what do you see? What do you see when you walk through your house? What are the first things your eyes go to? What do you see when you look out of your windows? Walking into your office? Walking through the mall? How about the airport? Where do your eyes go first? Now think of how your view of what you see every day could change if you were in a wheelchair. How does your perception change when viewing the world from that height? We've all heard the phrase 'perception is reality.' Well, I now had a new perception and vision of the world, and therefore it had become a changing reality. I now saw things very differently.

One day, Darlene arrived in my room, and we started my day business as usual. She went through the regular routine of rummaging through my belongings, tossing me the clothes I had ready and throwing my shoes and socks into my lap. With a larger-than-life smile, she watched as I got ready for the day, evaluating my every move. Needing her help to pull my shirt over my head, I was finally dressed. I just needed to complete the final hurdle—those dreaded shoes and socks. Being painstakingly slow, I finally completed this basic task with my heart pumping, a major head rush and sweat pouring from my head. It was a lengthy process for me just to get dressed, but I could finally do it virtually solo, with just the most minimal assistance. This was a huge WIN! Darlene, who was still smiling, reached over, grabbed the placard from my chair, placed the last remaining green dot on my card and said, "CONGRATULATIONS! YOU'VE LOST YOUR WHEELS!"

Pushing the wheelchair aside, she said it again, "You've lost your wheels. We will no longer be using the chair in your therapy sessions." *Wait, what?* I thought to myself. This was a major piece of news for me. As excited as I was that this could be a reality, I was still very nervous about this prospect. As much as I wanted out of that wheelchair for good, it was still a safety net for me. I was still very unstable, and although I had made much progress, was it enough that I could move forward without my wheelchair? I was about to find out. Darlene looked at the door, still wearing that smile, and with confidence and authority in her voice she said, "Let's go," and headed for the hallway. This was my moment. What I had been working so hard to achieve. My heart started to race with excitement and adrenaline.

With my game face on, I started to make my move. We slowly walked in the direction of the door. This was a surreal moment. For the first time in three months, I was taking steps from my room out into the hallway. This was a game-changing moment. I felt like a giant and felt like I could touch the ceiling with the top of my head. My body seemed to fill the space around me. I felt as if everything was closing in on me and the hallway looked like it went on forever. The ceiling tiles were closer, the walls were tighter, and the lights seemed brighter. The chair rails, light switches and paintings on the walls all looked so different from my new perspective. It was a familiar hallway that I had been traveling every day, but now it felt completely different. Like being in the mirrored house at an amusement park, I felt like a flagpole or Stretch Armstrong, taking very slow steps with my gangly and unstable limbs dangling along the way. The distance from my eyes to the floor seemed endless and the carpet pattern looked completely different. As I walked with Darlene at my side, I was in amazement at everything around me. When we passed a hospital room with the door open and I could see a glimpse of a patient, I thought they must believe they were looking back at a giant. I was so proud and gained confidence with each step, motivated by every smiling face. In my own special way of visualization, I felt as if everyone was cheering for me. This motivated me to keep going. Not only was my visual observation completely different but my blood pressure and internal organs were also working overtime trying to play catch up. With a head rush and sweat rolling down one side of my forehead, (the other side of my body wasn't yet sweating at all), I walked to the end of the hallway until I reached the elevator area and nurses' station. There she was, June. The woman whom that beautiful and cheerful voice belonged to now stood in full view of me. Until that point, I could only recognize her by the top of her head. Now I could see her full and beautiful face to go along with that wonderful voice I heard each day. I'll never forget her smile as now she looked *up* at me. I was now looking down at her instead of looking up to the top of her head. For the first time I saw the person behind the voice as she stared at me with an expression of excitement and joy. She was ecstatic to see me actually walking to that elevator. I don't think she will ever realize the impact she had on me during that time of my life. Her small but precious gift of acknowledging me each day played more of a role in my psyche than I can even describe. And I am sure she has done that for every patient who has been a part of her responsibility. As I headed to the elevator, I stared at the same floor buttons I had pushed every day during those weeks/months I had been at rehab. This time I was reaching down to press them instead of reaching up. How interesting this is such a powerful memory for me. It is an example of those everyday moments we have and which we never even think about. Until something changes your ability to move through those moments in the way you are conditioned to. Something so insignificant can truly show you how fragile each of us really is in this life and how little control we actually have in the guarantee of our future. Even getting into the elevator felt like an entirely new experience. Not only did it all look so different to me, but I was also very dizzy as we rode it to the first floor. Hopefully my body would soon adjust to this experience. We arrived at our destination and the doors opened. I had arrived at what seemed an entirely new world. Feeling like a powerful giant, I stepped into the room. Debby was the first person I saw. Her huge smile was visible from across the room. As I approached, she said, "Look at you!" With a small tear in her eye, she gave me a hug. The other patients who were in the room and who knew me had stopped what they were working on to witness this monumental occasion. As I walked through the room, I started to hear cheering and clapping from them. They were so excited to see me walking again. I think back on this and reflect how rare of an occasion this probably was for someone who had been in my condition. It also makes me think of all those others who were with me not only on my journey but also on their own journeys. And how many of those same people did not reach the same result I did, having the ability to walk on their own once again. This is a sobering thought.

This day was filled with many 'firsts' and I was consumed with hope. This was a new beginning for me, one which marked a goal in my journey I had been working so hard to achieve. It was a day I will never forget giving me such an overwhelming feeling of accomplishment and empowerment. Those slow, unsteady steps I was taking independently established a new focus in my routine for therapy. It was a pivotal moment for my life ahead and I was ready to tackle whatever needed to come next to keep advancing. I was a far better version of myself than I had been entering that rehab center weeks before. And I was nowhere near the end of pushing myself to new heights. In my mind, my progress still to come was limitless. Now that I was classified as independent from the wheelchair, that did not mean I was completely free from the chair. The goal was to continue improving my mobility and to walk as much as I could while carefully maneuvering new obstacles and diversions without regressing in my conditioning. I continued working through various therapy sessions, including increased time in the pool. As I moved closer to my intended release date, I learned what my 'final exam' would entail. That would be a weekend stay in the 'apartment' within the rehab center. That's right. An apartment. It was a space designed to simulate all that would be required to live at home independently. We made the plan and scheduled the date for when Shelly would join me for two days in this setting. We would be on our own, making our way through those days as if I had already returned home. As exciting a thought as this was, it was also a very daunting thought. It was strange to think of leaving this new environment which had become my cocoon of healing. In the rehab center I was safe. The people here knew me and knew what I had been through. They were significant and instrumental in every aspect of my life. If I had trouble, they were right there to help me. They had seen me and walked with me through some of my darkest days. They were there with me through the most vulnerable, embarrassing and challenging times of my life. I felt safe and cared for. It was also a safety zone as the other patients here were also going through similar scenarios in their own struggles. They understood what I was going through and how hard it was when your life changed so quickly and unexpectedly. They understood not only the physical challenges but also the mental and emotional ones. I was with a community of people who had shared in some of the most intimate moments of my life and which others would never understand unless they went through something similar. It was a positive place where the focus was on the future and each small win was celebrated, regardless of how seemingly insignificant it was to the outside world. I was not sure I was ready to go back to the world where other people did not understand this. Where the pace was so fast, and people did not want to take the time or pay attention to someone like me who was still discovering their own body and abilities once again. It was an unsettling and scary thought. But that weekend in the apartment? I was ready for that!

The date was set, and Shelly and I were both excited and ready for the test. Shelly was extra excited, as she had been anxiously awaiting the time when I could finally come home. Once I had been transferred to Wake Rehab, Shelly had returned to work full time. The stores had continued to stay extremely busy since their grand opening weekends with sales climbing and teams growing and transitioning. She had been working relentless hours trying to stay on top of her responsibilities at work while at the same time, coming to see me multiple times each day. She would come and visit me before going to work in the morning if time would allow and would always come to see me in the evenings. If she was able to, she would even take a meal break in the middle of the day and come to see me then. It had been a constant juggling act and she was pretty exhausted. She was ready to have me home again. My brother, Bob, and his now ex-wife, Julie, had come down to visit toward the end of my stay at rehab. They happened to still be in town during our 'weekend in the apartment.' We got a movie, brought in some pizza and just had fun, catching up and enjoying each other's company in a more natural setting. I almost forgot I was still in rehab. As it got later into the evening, it was time for them to return to our apartment and Shelly and I to check out our new 'digs' for the next 24+ hours. The bedroom was typical and simple with a bathroom attached to it. This bathroom was anything but typical. It was a huge space, allowing more than enough room for wheelchairs and other equipment to maneuver around the space. Hanging from the ceiling was probably every piece of adaptive equipment you could think of. It is amazing the diversity of resources available to assist people in all types of situations of health and wellness. Shelly went in to use the bathroom, and what happened next can only be described by her:

I went in to use the bathroom. As I was sitting on the toilet, I was looking around at all the medical supplies and equipment in this room. It was fascinating and kind of overwhelming how much was on display. There was a sink to my left and a walk-in shower to my right. As I was looking around, I heard a noise to my right and caught something out of the corner of my eye. I looked over and had to blink a couple of times to ensure I was seeing what I thought I was seeing. Out of the drain in the shower were emerging little antennae and spindly little legs. What the heck is that?! *I thought. As I continued to watch in horror, a creature emerged from the drain and scurried up the wall of the shower. Behind that first one, more were coming. I freaked out! I screamed, jumped up and scrambled as fast as I could out of that bathroom. I ran into the bedroom and jumped on the bed where Michael was lying down. I started jumping up and down on the bed, pointing at the bathroom and screaming and yelling for him to do something. In my panic I looked down to see poor Michael, bobbing around on the mattress while I was jumping up and down. He was looking at me with this bewildered and kind of horrified look and asking me what the heck was wrong. "There are crazy creatures coming out of the drain in the shower! You have to do something! We have to kill them. Right now. There are a bunch coming out of the drain!" I shouted at him in despair. "What do you want me to do about it?" he asked. "I can barely move." It dawned on me I was in a panic and asking a paralyzed guy to go in and kill all these creatures.* Crap! *I thought. I grabbed the phone and tossed it to him, asking him to call someone to come in and take care of these creatures. I then raced back into the bathroom and started looking for something I could kill them with. I grabbed a bunch of cleaning chemicals and towels and headed toward the shower. Screaming and crying every step of the way, I used the towel to swat the creatures off the side of the shower to the floor and then I turned on the water to flush them back down the drain. I then started pouring the various chemicals I had grabbed, including bleach, down that drain. I could hear those creatures screaming as the chemicals made their way through the pipes. My panic haze started to clear a bit and I looked down at what I had in my hands.* What was I doing? *I thought to myself. I was mixing all these chemicals together. I could be making a bomb! I then ran the water again and heard more screaming and screeching from those bugs. I left the water running, ran toward the door and grabbed more towels on the way. I left the bathroom, slamming the door and taking rolled-up towels and placed them at the bottom of the door. Meanwhile, Michael had gotten in touch with someone who was sending a maintenance guy down to try to take care of the problem. He did come to our room to try and take care of the bugs, but I was not buying that the problem was solved. I don't know how I slept a minute that night as I was terrified to even step onto the floor. I picked up our belongings, put them on top of tables and chairs and stayed on that bed with my eyes glued to the bathroom door. I kept the towels along the bottom the entire night. I was counting down the minutes until we could get out of there. So much for a romantic weekend in 'the apartment.'*

How we made it through that night I have no idea. We were more than ready to get out of there as soon as we could the next day. Beyond the whole bug fiasco, we did well, handling and maneuvering actions and activities I would be encountering once back at home. Recapping the experience with my therapists, they were quite impressed with how we were able to work through the traumatic moments of the 'creature experience' together. Although I must admit that was pretty much all Shelly handling that problem, as I was of little assistance during that time. At least we knew she could handle more than she wanted to handle in a crisis situation. And I definitely had the ability to calm her back down and help her realize that together, we could accomplish anything.

Shelly had been working hard at home, preparing for my return. Initially, we thought I would be returning in a wheelchair, and she had been fighting with our apartment complex to be able to move to a handicap accessible apartment on the first floor. We lived on the third floor in a complex with no elevators. As I had progressed during my time in rehab, we had started to realize that potentially, I would be able to walk out of rehab. That I would no longer have a need for a wheelchair. So, she had stalled her action to move, and we decided we would stay in our current apartment. Hopefully this was a wise decision on our part. My therapists knew this was our situation, so we concentrated heavily on improving my balance and using the stairs and continuing to strengthen all the muscles involved with being able to do that. The time was near as my final day at rehab was approaching. I had one last important task to accomplish before I left. And I needed the help of my new friends, my therapists. As things were all coming together, I found out the people directly responsible for my recovery had been conspiring behind the scenes to do something special for me and Shelly. The team knew that while I had been in the hospital, I had proposed to Shelly. They also knew I had borrowed my grandmother's ring from my sister Kathleen to use for the proposal as a temporary option. They were fully aware that a top priority for me was to buy Shelly an engagement ring. One meant just for her. One of the therapists had a connection and an idea that included my going on a little field trip. They arranged to have a special van arrive during one of my therapy sessions, and with four of the therapists joining me on this excursion, we carefully loaded up the van and hit the road. This was a complete surprise, and I had no idea where we were going. It was my first time back on the road other than ambulance rides. I was now sitting upright in a middle seat, secured by a seat belt and sitting between two therapists whose job it was to sit close enough to me so I would not fall over. My core muscles had not yet been fine-tuned, so falling over was a strong possibility. We arrived in a more historic area of Raleigh which had a few stores to shop. We exited the van and proceeded to a door with a security entrance. This was the entrance to a jewelry store which was in what looked like a residential building. It was very discreet and inconspicuous. Upon entering, I was introduced to the owner. He was a friend of one of my therapists. He had been told a bit about my story and the purpose as to why we were there. My team knew that my intentions were to officially propose to Shelly on my own two feet with a ring I had picked out specially for her. I could not believe they had gone to such an effort to help me with this endeavor. I was very emotional that they would take the time and effort to assist me in this way. They were emotional as well and so happy to play a role in this part of my journey. I sat down with the owner of the store and personally designed a beautiful ring for Shelly. My vision was for Shelly and me to return to the place where we had fallen in love with North Carolina, Wrightsville Beach. I wanted to return to the pier, that first place we had landed the previous year while on vacation. I wanted this spot, with the backdrop of the gorgeous Atlantic Ocean, to be the location where I could get down on one knee and propose to her. Spending some time discussing Shelly and her style, as well as my vision for a ring, we created a design plan for the ring. Now I needed to be patient, let the jeweler work his magic and prepare for a very significant occasion ahead. But first, I needed to finish my final days at rehab.

TWELVE

YOU GAVE ME STRENGTH

But those who hope in the Lord will renew their strength.

They will soar on wings like eagles; they will run and not

grow weary; they will walk and not be faint.

—*Isaiah 40:31*

Strength comes from many different sources. Shelly. She is my love. She gives me strength. Her presence in my mind gives me hope and a reason to live. At the very time I needed our Creator the most, I not only cried out for Him, but I also cried out and claimed my love for my Shelly. I believe love heals wounds and gives you strength when you need more than your own physical body. During the toughest times in our lives, love is the energy that helps us move forward. It comes from God and in the form of relationships, through family, friends and sometimes strangers. In spirit and in mind, love helps us to *become* and creates the foundation to make us believe anything is possible. Remember, (John 3:16) 'For God so loved the world that he gave his one and only son, that whoever believes in him shall not perish but have eternal life.'

There are so many interesting, enlightening and in-depth conversations I have had with people since my accident. My accident provided a door to open into conversations I may not have otherwise had with people. It has provided me with more opportunities to showcase God's goodness and grace and the strength He empowers us with. One of these conversations happened later in my recovery process. Shelly and I were visiting with friends whom she grew up with. I had met them only a few times, but they were a lot of fun and accepted me into their group from the beginning. They had been a huge support to us both, especially to Shelly, after my accident. They all lived in Michigan but had stayed very connected to us since we had moved to North Carolina. During our first trip back to Michigan after my accident and being released from rehab, we all got together one night. Entering the living room, I sat down next to David, the husband of one of Shelly's childhood friends. We started talking and I quickly discovered he was very curious about my accident and had many questions for me regarding my faith and beliefs. After talking for a while, he leaned into me with piercing eyes and an intense gaze and presented me with a loaded question. This was a question that challenged my faith and had us quickly moving into deeper conversation. He asked, "If God loves everyone, how did He let this happen to you?" I am sure you have heard this question before or maybe even have thought it yourself. He went on to question why so many people are suffering in this world and wondered how, if God is so good, He could allow bad things to happen to good people. He went on to ask, "If God is real, why would He allow you to be injured and allow you to have seizures?" I must admit, these questions caught me off guard and I was a bit uncomfortable at first. But my strong faith and belief that His goodness had helped me through so much in my life had me prepared to answer at least some of his questions. I politely responded with a challenge back to him. I asked, "Why not me?" Just maybe God had allowed me to experience challenges in my life and was preparing me for something great despite them. Maybe He wanted me to trust in His plan. I believe He was preparing me to become a better version of myself. Maybe I was BECOMING the person He needed me to be for greater things to come. It may not be obvious with the damage done to my body, but my mind and spirit are strong. As our conversation continued, my level of gratitude grew even stronger. I had this opportunity to share with someone the depth of love God has for us and how the strength of our belief in Him can carry us through the toughest of times. In a strange way I was reminding myself that trauma can be a stepping-stone to something special, and the strength we discover along the way is there for us to discover. It is up to us how we interpret different situations and how we can utilize challenging experiences and tough moments to gain strength.

Without our faith and our Creator's goodness, I believe the outcome of our trials would have been drastically different. But I also strongly believe that along with faith comes hard work, discipline and a strong, positive mindset. Each one of us has the ability to form our own belief system and have our own spiritual journey. There is power in being able to see the blessings around you and to understand that everything you see is being perfectly aligned for you to use in future trials. Over the years and throughout my recovery, the most often asked question has been, "How did you learn to walk again? Where did you find the strength to recover?"

These questions are asked as if I had discovered the perfect formula. I do not have all the answers for sure. But I do know my faith has carried me through and the power of prayer, my belief in God and a positive mindset are directly linked to the fact that I am walking today.

In a strange way, because of my injury I became hypersensitive and more aware of my surroundings. When I found myself reliant on others to help me with everyday needs, it changed how I saw the world. I had time to think deeply of all the things so many of us take for granted. Basic things like giving a hug, holding a spoon, brushing your teeth, shaving, being able to take a shower, lifting an arm or taking one small step took on greater meaning. You begin to see everything around you, including seemingly insignificant movements, as a blessing. I found this to be true in every activity and for the many acts of kindness that surrounded me. I hope to this day we show kindness to others in the way we live our lives. One could say, having grown up in a strict Catholic environment, I was religious. But my relationship with God has not been about adhering to religious rules or being tied to a specific building I choose to worship in. Through my faith and understanding, I believe the Bible is an instructional manual to guide each of us through life. Our faith and relationship with God are centered in our actions. My relationship with God is strong and He is with me everywhere I go. I cannot begin to imagine going through the trials I have been through without God next to me, walking me through those toughest moments. Over the years, I have discovered that some of my deepest prayers, thoughts and conversations with God happen on the back of our tandem bike or while I am running through our neighborhood in the darkness of the night or during my drive while commuting to work. My relationship with God brings me peace, a sense of calm and a confidence that

I can overcome whatever it is that happens in my life, as long as He is with me. Going through the trials I have gone through has only strengthened and deepened my relationship with God. In turn, He gives me the strength to overcome.

My team in rehab also gave me strength. I was so fortunate to have people like Darlene who believed in me and pushed me beyond my comfort zone. One day I received an extra dose of inspiration, and I was reminded even Superman is human. As I was finishing up a physical therapy session, Darlene came over and said there was something she wanted to show me. Tired from the workout and needing a rest, I was grateful for the break. She wheeled me into the lobby where there was a TV mounted on the wall. Darlene said there was some breaking news I needed to see. I looked up and saw the unbelievable. There had been an accident where a man had been thrown from a horse as he attempted a jump. He was seriously injured and had suffered a spinal cord injury. As I watched in amazement, I realized that man was Christopher Reeve. He was the original actor who famously played Superman in the movies. He had suffered a very serious high-level spinal cord injury. It was sad news and confirmed these types of traumatic injuries could happen to anyone, at any time. Car and diving accidents are the most common causes of spinal cord injuries. Now I was watching someone else, besides myself, who had gone through a freak accident which resulted in a devastating spinal cord injury. And this was Superman! I was appreciative that Darlene thought it was important for me to see this story unfolding, and in a strange way, it motivated me to keep working even harder. I had a complete day of therapy in front of me and I was motivated more than ever to work harder and continue to make progress. Christopher Reeve's story gave me additional strength to power through the most difficult activities and exercises as I worked toward my goals.

On another occasion, on a different day, I was working out on weight machines. I was in front of a weight machine doing cable exercises with no weight attached, working on my triceps. As I worked out, I had a visit from my doctor, Dr. O'Brien. He was accompanied by a young woman, and he asked if we could have a conversation. Of course I said yes, and we moved over to a quiet part of the rehab floor. As they sat down, this woman was introduced to me. Dr. O'Brien explained she had been a previous patient of his and had suffered a spinal cord injury like mine, a C5 incomplete injury. Now she was coming back to the hospital to share her story with other patients and to offer additional encouragement to those who were still in the depths of their own struggle. Looking at her, I could not believe it. She looked fantastic and had limited mobility issues, which were barely notice-able as she shared her story with me. This was a heartwarming, motivating experience and a pivotal moment in my recovery. Again, like Christopher Reeve's story, I was being reminded that I was not alone. These types of injuries happen every day to real people. She gave me hope and a reason to believe that there is 'life after injury.' There were many blessings to be found, she explained, as she was still, years after her injury, continuing to discover her own and becoming stronger every day. Dr. O'Brien shared how well she had transitioned into the real world but emphasized how hard she had to work at it each day. He went on to explain to me that the daily therapies I was currently involved in would need to become a regular part of my life going forward. My progress would be reliant on working hard every day. I would always have to keep moving and challenging myself for ongoing improvement. At this point, it was yet to be determined the outcome of how much return I would have in my limbs. The development of the small, fine nerves and muscles in my hands and feet and lessening the weakness in my arms and legs would be my biggest opportunities in the long term. Improvements would be gradual and the continuation of that recovery beyond rehab would be dependent upon me. This conversation was one of those 'move it or lose it' conversations and one which I will never forget. It filled me with gratitude for the progress I had made and gave me additional inspiration and strength to continue. This stranger, who took the time to talk with me and share her own experience from her heart, created a clear picture that the road ahead would not be easy, but the hard work would be worth it.

With all that was going on, it could have been very easy for me to become discouraged. But these stories only fueled my fire and gave me greater focus. God had perfectly aligned these incidents to be in my path so I would gain additional strength along the way. But what about the people around me? Surely my condition and injury had taken a huge toll on Shelly even though she did not show it. What about each one of my family members? How did they stay so strong while continuing to motivate me? What was giving them strength through their feelings, thoughts and concerns for me, not knowing what the future would hold for me? They all continued to share their love with me through notes, cards, phone calls, visits and taking detailed notes of my progress along the way. I am sure each of these actions gave them encouragement knowing they were taking action to help me in their own unique way. Looking back, I truly believe my family, especially Shelly, had a tougher time than I did. I had a huge support team helping me. They had each other but the geographic distance challenged them to deal with much of the unknown themselves.

Shortly after my injury, Shelly came across a book which would offer an additional source of hope and inspiration for my entire family. Being an avid reader, she found a book in the hospital gift shop called *Rise and Walk: The Trial and Triumph of Dennis Byrd*. It was perfect, as it was a story very similar to my own. Dennis Byrd had been a professional football player who played for the New York Jets and had suffered a C5 spinal cord injury during a game while airing live on TV. Later, his story was turned into an ABC Movie of the Week. It was a story of turning tragedy into triumph. The book was quickly purchased by many in my family and shared with others. It was a story filled with possibilities and gave our family, including me, hope. It was filled with stories of strength Dennis Byrd had from his faith and family and was like my own situation in which I was learning the power of my faith along the way. Back in Livonia, my sister Kathy walked into her kitchen one day and found her son Shaun, a first grader, sitting at the kitchen table writing a letter. She said, "Shaun, what are you doing?" He replied, "I'm writing a letter to Dennis Byrd." With a look of amazement, she said, "You are writing to a professional football player?" She was stunned. He had no idea how he was going to get his letter to Dennis Byrd, but he was determined to tell him what happened to his Uncle Mike. Proud and touched by his love for his uncle and determination to share his story, Kathleen helped him complete his mission. She did some research and found an address to the Dennis Byrd Foundation, which is where they sent the letter. Not only would Dennis Byrd receive the letter, but he would also send his own letter back to me in response. He also included an autographed copy of his book for me. Shaun's letter and this action he took will be something I will cherish for the rest of my life. The letter and response from Dennis Byrd would later be displayed, along with his football card, in a frame on the wall of my office when I returned to work. Shaun's letter and the encouragement it gave me inspired the people on my team every day and gave each of us the drive to keep moving forward. It was a reminder that accidents happen, but the blessings and lessons which come from them are more important.

Shaun's Letter:

Dear Dennis Byrd,

My uncle Mike was in a car accident. He hit two cows. A 1500lbs mom cow and a baby. He has plates in his neck like you. Now he is out of the hospital. But he used to play soccer with me. But I hope he still can. At first all he could only move was his eyes. I never wrote a football player before. Maybe you could send him a picture.

Thank you,

Shaun Fyffe

Dennis Byrd's response was accompanied with this amazing prayer penned on the first page of the book he sent to me. It is a message with a mindset which I continue to share with others around me who are in need. It speaks to our spirit and teaches us that regardless of the physical results from a trauma, recovery and power begin between our ears.

The blessings that you discover through your personal trials often are not revealed in your body, but in your mind and spirit. In the quiet times of the night, remember-somewhere I will be saying a prayer for you. Somehow, someway, God will make your trial a blessing. Finding the blessing is up to you.

—Dennis Byrd

Former, New York Jet #90

THIRTEEN

A NEW NORMAL

But he said to me, "My grace is sufficient for you, for my
power is made perfect in weakness." Therefore, I will boast
all the more gladly about my weakness, so that Christ's
power may rest on me.

—2 Corinthians 12:9 NIV

What is normal today does not mean it is your forever. As we started
to pack and organize my belongings to leave the rehab center, a strange
feeling washed over me. I felt like I was leaving part of my family. The place
I had called home for the past few weeks and months was about to become
a memory. Etched into my brain would be the comfort and care I had
received during my time at Wake Medical and the significance the experience and the people working there had in helping to put my body and my
life back together. The Red Team had felt like family to me, but it was now

time to say goodbye. I would continue with outpatient rehab and put into action the teachings from my therapists. I would not forget the many tough love conversations I had shared with my team. The thought of going back out into the real world was scary. It felt a bit overwhelming to be leaving my safety net. Discharge paperwork and evaluations were completed, and goodbyes ensued with staff and patients alike. I was leaving with the realization that I was walking out of rehab a changed person from the one who had entered the facility, both inside and out. As Shelly and I organized and prepared to leave, I noticed that a new patient had just moved in across the hall. As I saw this older woman lying in her bed resting, she looked over in our direction with a friendly smile and gentle eyes. She was alone in her room. As we loaded up our cart to transfer my personal belongings down to the elevator, I picked up a guardian angel from my bedside table. It had been sent to me in one of the many cards I had received, and it was one of the last things left to pack up. Something about this sweet little lady tugged at our hearts. Before we walked down the hallway, we went over to say hello and to meet her. She was very open to talking to us and grateful to have us visit with her for a little bit. Before leaving, we asked her if we could pray with her. I also told her I had a gift I wanted to leave with her. She gently smiled, agreed to pray with us and reached out her hands toward me. I placed the guardian angel into her cupped hands, and she closed her fingers around it. She lay back on her bed cradling that little angel and closed her eyes. She had such a sweet and beautiful smile on her face as she held it to her heart. We felt very honored to have had that moment with her and felt it was a sign and gift from God for us to be able to connect with her in that way at that moment. After our short visit, we wished her well and made our way down that long hallway toward the elevator.

As the door opened to the main floor lobby, I remember clutching Shelly's hand as we slowly walked out of the elevator and into that space. We said goodbye to all we passed as we made our way out of the door and into the parking lot. As we approached our car I turned to glance back, overwhelmed with emotion. I was leaving a place that had made me stronger physically, mentally and emotionally. It had also acted as a safe haven for me, allowing me to heal in a safe and protected environment. While there, I never felt self-conscious in the way I walked, looked or struggled to complete movements and tasks. I was still weak, wearing my Philadelphia collar to stabilize my neck, decked out in fancy sweatpants and in need of a real shave and shower. I was far from looking my best. It was a surreal experience to be driving across town, back to the apartment I had not seen for months. I was more than a little bit apprehensive. We had a lot of work ahead of us and the realization hit me hard that now, my continued progress and future ahead would be dependent upon my own actions. It was up to me to continue to carry the torch of my 'rehabilitation' I would be working on for the rest of my life.

Arriving home to our apartment, we stood at the bottom of the stairs. We lived on the third floor and there was no elevator ride to make the ascent to get to our door any easier. I was so grateful to God I did not return home in a wheelchair. But now I was looking up at the three flights of stairs in front of me, wondering if I truly would be able to make the climb. With Shelly by my side and holding onto me, we started up those stairs one step at a time. It was slow going and I felt wobbly and unsteady, but the higher we went, the more confident I became. We finally made it to the top landing and we stood at the door, ready to go in. Emotions ran high through my body and I started to cry. I was home. I was so grateful to be home, on my own two feet, with Shelly at my side and our beautiful kitty on the other side of that door waiting for us. Before going in, I knelt to kiss the ground. The tears rolled from my eyes, down my cheeks and onto the concrete, leaving wet spots behind. Shelly helped me up, crying with me and together, we opened the door and walked inside. It was as beautiful and spotless as I remembered it. As I walked in, I immediately spotted him—Kiki. Our very special and gorgeous pure white cat staring at me with his piercing blue eyes. He looked at me and started crying out as he approached, walking between my legs and reaching up for me. His purr was music to my ears and so much better than the sounds and whirs of the hospital equipment I had left behind. I was back where I was supposed to be!

Having the ability to walk away from the rehabilitation center was an unbelievable gift. A day did not go by without me counting my blessings and being overwhelmed with gratitude. My 'new normal' had begun. We did not waste any time and the next day, Shelly and I went for a long walk. This was only the beginning of a new routine for us both. Movement became a necessity. As long as my legs, the gifts God had gifted me, allowed me to stand and walk, I was going to use them. But I was changed. As much as I was ready and we tried to return to life as we had known it before, I was physically and mentally changed. Diagnosed with weakness in all four limbs, I was unstable on my feet, walked with a limp and was currently sporting a not-so-sexy Philadelphia collar around my neck. I was sure people were thinking to themselves, *Holy Cow! What happened to that guy?* However, this did not deter me in any way. In fact, I embraced the moments when people stopped to ask me about my story and what had happened. I mean really, who has the opportunity to share a story about how they hit multiple cows and survived to talk about it? Not long after I had returned home, Shelly's sister Leslie came to visit. Shelly was back to work, and we were both grateful for me to have some help and company at home while Shelly was working. Leslie's visit was so good for us both for many reasons and it was great timing. She loves to walk and has a passion for moving your body every day. That endurance gene runs in Shelly's family! While Shelly was at work, Leslie and I had many great conversations during our walks around the apartment complex and in the time spent at the pool. In the evenings, we would all be together, catching up, sharing and discussing our plans for the future. We were so grateful to have Leslie with us and to have some family share this critical period with us. Many uncertainties lay ahead, but Shelly and I both knew a priority was our own health and well-being. For the first time in our lives, taking care of ourselves became a top priority and way of life for us both.

Walks around our apartment complex were fun and challenging for a while, but we started to outgrow them and needed a new and bigger challenge. We had picked up a great book which listed the state parks and many attractions throughout the state of North Carolina. It also listed the accessibility details so we could assess if it was the right place for us to visit or not. One spot grabbed our attention, the North Carolina Zoo located outside of Asheville. The NC Zoo is one of the largest natural habitat zoos in the country with miles of walking paths weaving throughout it. This sounded like a fantastic excursion to take, and we were ready to tackle it! So, we put the plans in place for our day trip. We may have underestimated just how big it was and how much walking was entailed to be able to make our way throughout the entire zoo. When we arrived, we immediately noticed how full the parking lot was. There was a zoo transportation vehicle which took people from the parking lot to the entrance. It was a busy place and it was my first time being around a large crowd. We had not parked that far away from the entrance, so we decided to walk across the parking lot. As we entered, we noticed many people were using scooters and wheelchairs to move throughout the environment. Having just been given the gift of mobility to use my legs once again, there was no way I was not going to walk this park. It was a gorgeous day, and we were so happy and excited to have the opportunity to be there. The animal lover that she is, Shelly was more excited than I was. The weakness radiating in both of my legs and throughout my body was sending up a message, *don't overdo it.* I ignored it and we set off for an amazing day. As we walked, we became more and more energized that we were actually doing it. The paths throughout the zoo were windy and curvy, sloping up and down throughout the property. The more we walked, the stronger I felt. We were almost giddy that I was able to do this. I felt empowered with every step. As we had feelings of excitement and elation, we walked behind many able-bodied people who were complaining every step of the way. They were too hot, too tired, their legs hurt, it was taking too long to walk, whatever. Whenever we would hear this, we would look at each other and start laughing as we made our way around and past them. They had no idea how different their lives could be. They had no idea of how many people I had left behind in the rehab center who would never walk again. I was in pain and fatigued but there was no way in hell I was going to stop. This popular NC tourist destination did not disappoint, and we saw just about every animal from around the globe represented there. The good news? We did not see any cows.

The fact that we did not have an elevator to our third-floor apartment was not a problem for me; it was actually an unforeseen gift. Because

I was forced to walk up and down those stairs to leave the apartment, my legs and stamina strengthened faster and to a greater degree. Walking became part of my daily routine, and I was so grateful to be able to do it. Soon it was time for me to return to the hospital for a follow-up visit. I would be meeting with my original neurosurgeons who performed my surgeries, Dr. Macedo and Dr. Guarino. I had been making great progress and was eager to be evaluated. Wearing a Philadelphia collar to keep my neck stabilized had become very uncomfortable in the heat of summer. I had to wear it every day, to bed as well. I was hoping to get the sign-off to not have to wear this collar any longer. The primary objective for this visit was to evaluate not only my progress but also how well the incision in my neck had healed. This visit meant we were going back to Nash General Hospital for the first time since leaving after my accident. The doctors' offices were in an adjacent medical building to the hospital, but we also planned to visit the nurses at the hospital who had been so instrumental in my recovery and experience there. As we entered the office building, I remember feeling very accomplished. This encounter could have been so different in many ways, and I was overwhelmed with gratitude. As Shelly and I walked down the hallway in the direction of the office, I heard a voice say, "Holy Cow! That's not Michael Warner!" As we walked into the office, both doctors were there with huge smiles on their faces. They were pleasantly shocked at how well I was doing. After briefly catching up on recent experiences, they got to work for my appointment. They did an evaluation of my gait and walking technique, analyzing how my body was responding to the movement, pivots and turns. Next, they slowly removed my collar and the bandage that covered my incision. It was exhilarating to see their expressions as they admired their own handy work. The good news was the incision was looking fantastic and I was healing better than expected. They were very impressed with my progress. It was difficult to put into words but also so important for us to express to them the amount of gratitude we had for their skill and efforts. As Shelly and I left that office, I will never forget their reactions to me on that day. It was rare and somewhat shocking for someone with my level of injury to return to them walking. It gave them hope and inspiration to witness my healing. It was also very rare for someone who had been through what I had been through, facing an uncertain future, yet show so much gratitude to be in the position I was in. We wanted to ensure those doctors knew just how grateful we were for their skill and efforts in responding to my injury and physical challenges. And the icing on the cake? I was able to remove that darn Philadelphia collar. Yes!

For the next two months Shelly and I had a strong focus on getting back to a new regular routine. We also recognized the significance to stay focused on our own well-being. We believed that my accident, in a strange way, was a reminder to slow down and to not be so consumed with work and not take each other for granted. We needed to ensure we did not lose the lesson in all of this to stay connected with what really is important in this life. Work should not take the #1 spot on our priority list. This would be easier said than done because of the passion we had for our professions and company. But we worked hard to make some necessary changes. The first step was to stay as active as possible. So, we decided to join a gym. The doctor had told me I would need to stay active and continue my own form of 'rehab' for the rest of my life. Shelly continued to remind me that working out is important for anyone and everyone, but it was especially important for me to maintain the use of my limbs and muscles going forward. Our workouts were for life, not just a good workout to get in shape. I had lost a lot of weight while in the hospital and rehab and I walked with a defined limp. I was a little intimidated going into the gym, wondering what others would think of me. Would they see me as weak, not measuring up to the other fit and heavy-lifting guys who worked out in the gym? But Shelly was the first to remind me of how far I had come. How far we had come together. We were only just beginning this next part of our journey and I had a story like no other. Reminding myself of this gave me the strength and courage to get into that gym and give it all I had because I was and am an overcomer. Nothing was going to stop me, especially the opinions of others. I must be honest though. It is a strange feeling to be in a gym atmosphere with able-bodied people all around who have no idea I had been paralyzed and only recently started walking again. It was embarrassing for me to be doing cable exercises with little or no weight on the machine. Yet, in a strange way this also motivated me to work harder. I must admit, I never left a machine with only 5 or 10 pounds on it. After I cleaned it off, I'd pull the pin and add 40 or 50 pounds to the machine so the next person would be impressed with how much I could lift. It was just a fun way that made me feel like at that time in my life, regardless of my fitness and strength level, I was still strong, capable and fit.

As time progressed it became apparent that my workouts and long walks were paying off. I was becoming stronger and had vastly improved balance. My outpatient rehab doctors had finally cleared me to go back to work. This was fantastic news, as one of the main goals I had been focused on post-rehab was getting back to work as quickly as possible. I still needed to work at strengthening my hands and improving the dexterity of my fingers because those fine, small muscles were taking their time to heal. But

I was making progress. With the thought of my position at work and the skill, experience and creativity I had for my profession, I decided to do a project which would simultaneously benefit me at work while also helping to improve the functioning of my hands and fingers. I decided to write a training manual for my teams. It was the perfect motivation to get me back into the right mindset I would need. My intent was not only to help myself but also to create a tool which would be useful for others in my field.

When the big day finally arrived for me to return to work, I was nervous. Target had been very accommodating, yet they were eager to have me back even though I was not yet 100%. I felt blessed in so many ways, but I also felt weak regarding many typical everyday tasks. I still had severe nerve and muscle damage, weakness in all four limbs and hot and cold sensation differences on both sides of my body. Looking at me you would not have known it. I was discovering the 'new' me and I did not share my apprehensions about returning to work with anyone except Shelly. As a matter of fact, until this very moment writing this book, I have never fully expressed what I was really feeling. I felt weak and 'less than.' Understanding the job at hand and the responsibilities of it, I did not want to get hurt. The thoughts of catching shoplifters again, putting myself in stressful and unpredictable situations like that had me fearful I could re-injure my neck. I was nervous. Yet these feelings were and are not what define me. I knew it was a blessing to have regained my mobility and I was grateful in so many ways. I just needed to keep in perspective my body was not the same as it had been that last day of work. The day of my accident. I spent decades as an athlete and had been confident in my abilities and expertise in the security realm. The reality was that my position at Target presented many stressful situations both as a corporate executive leader and physically, identifying and resolving internal and external theft and fraud. I had spent my entire career as a confident young, strong professional. I took a lot of pride in my accomplishments. With my years of experience and knowledge of how to successfully handle stressful, often potentially dangerous situations, I knew it was going to be far more challenging now after my accident. I also had my seizures to consider, as stress can be a trigger for seizures. Although I had spent my entire career managing my seizures and did so successfully under extreme pressures, now I was a little concerned with my new level of limitations. My confidence was shaken. The only way to overcome this was to get back in the action.

Regardless of my concerns I was determined and extremely grateful that I had a position to go back to. My mission and intention were simple, to do exactly what I had always done. Be the best of the best. To protect people and property without being a distraction and to be a seamless extension of a profitable business. To accommodate my return to work, Target made some adjustments so that I could return to a store in Raleigh, closer to our house. Shelly, who had opened and was currently working in the store they intended me to return to, would transfer across town to the highest volume store in the state. It was a perfect fit because they had a need and an opening for someone in her position. So back I went. I remember the day I returned, clutching my carry case by my side as I proudly walked across the parking lot with my new limp. I could not wait to get back to work and be a part of a great team once again. My identity was tied to my profession and what I was able to accomplish in the career that I had. I wanted to believe that my accident and injury had been a test that our Creator had allowed in our lives. Now it was time to show the world that I was literally a walking miracle because of God. I was ready!

As I entered my new office, I could feel that something was off. Was it just my nerves acting up? As I opened the door, I was stunned. The store's executive team, whom Shelly had worked so closely with from the beginning, had wanted me to feel comfortable and welcomed upon my return. So they thought they would be funny with a creative way to break the ice. The entire office was filled with COWS! Black and white was everywhere! Before I had arrived, they had gone into the store and found everything that Target sold that had a cow on it. Since it was September, this was easy with all of the Halloween decor in the store. The first thing I saw was the cow Halloween costume hanging from the camera monitors with the udders hanging in full glory. The entire office was filled with cows, clothing, cards and toys. The only thing missing was a wheelbarrow, shovel and the smell of manure. At least they spared me that! My new identity of being the 'cowboy' was enhanced. This fit right in with the cow cookie jar from Kathleen and the 10-gallon lid which Bob had brought to me. I immediately felt right at home with my new team!

One of the first big tests returning to work would be meeting my new boss. Before my transfer to the Carolinas, Target had to find a good replacement for me in Ann Arbor before my transfer would be approved. Because of the store's volume and history with the team, they were desperately searching for a great leader who had a lot of experience. They found the perfect person in San Diego, California, and he had quickly and seamlessly filled in behind me. During the timeframe of my accident and recovery, this same person would be promoted to a District Assets Protection Team Leader position and assigned to his own district. Not only was his name Mike but he was also promoted to our district! How about that for a coincidence? Mike was young, smart and skilled and had great leadership abilities. He was also a lot of fun. He was the type of boss everyone needs to have the experience of working with at least once in their lifetime. He was a visionary and had a great gift in making those around him better. We hit it off immediately. After taking some time to share the details behind my accident and recovery, I gave him the training manual I had written to strengthen my hands and fingers. This was oddly perfect timing as the company was working on enhancing training and development for our teams. Mike was so impressed with my expertise, vision and initiative with what I had created with my manual that he chose me and a peer to create another investigative manual for the company. This new manual ended up being used and distributed throughout our region. That was a great moment in validating my significance to my position and to the company. With pride, I very quickly fell back into routine with my position and new team, and I was quickly thrust back into a career-focused lifestyle.

First steps with PT Debbie behind me

The 'Cowboy' at Wake Rehab, Raleigh, NC

She said 'Yes'! St. Lucia, 1997

Dreams do come true!

She did it! 1st Marathon, 1988

Rock 'N' Roll San Diego Marathon, 2001

Glasgow, Scotland, 1999: with Shelly's Mom and Dad

Celebrating life and love in Salzburg, Austria, 2001
Left to right, Rich and Carol Brouwer, Shelly, me and Shelly's Mom and Dad

Christmas fun, 2012: left to right, Greg, Kathleen, Kent, Mary, Bob (back), me, Shelly

300-mile finish line! Michigan WAM 300, 2013   Team Jordan, Michigan WAM 300

Big surprise at the finish line-Bob!
2013, MI WAM 300

Celebrating 300 miles with
our moms

The celebration continues. Party in
the hood with Sarah, Mary and Mom

Dallas

Victory is sweeter with family:
Front, Shelly and me
back, Cameron, Mary, Kathleen, Jordan

Faith leading the way to the finish line
for the Dream Team
My first race ever:
Myrtle Beach Coastal 5K, 2018

2019

Our journey with Ainsley's Angels begins, 2015:
Kim 'Rooster' Rossiter, Shelly, me and Lori Rossiter

Running through life together: Run Gasparilla, 2018

Great friends and a Gasparilla 8K finish,
2018: left to right, Terry, Shelly, me Johnna

Pawsitivity-The journey continues, 2021

PART THREE
*BE*COME

FOURTEEN

STILL ME

I cried out, "I am slipping!" but your unfailing love, O
Lord, supported me. When doubts filled my mind, your
comfort gave me renewed hope and cheer.

—Psalms 94: 18–19

Returning to my career was easier than I expected, but I was not the same person. Physically, I had many new and permanent challenges I was still learning how to live my life with. The expectations had not changed for me to perform all aspects of my position with excellence, so it was critical I surrounded myself with a team of great people. I was blessed in so many ways, and over the years I had built a reputation for building great teams. A strength of mine was identifying talent and the training and development of my people. I had always known I would only be as good as the people I surrounded myself with. My teams were strong and confident in their skills and abilities. They were knowledgeable and good at what they did. We were known for our professionalism and creating a seamless presence in the stores. I maintained an active status in apprehending shoplifters and training my teams through leading by example in nonviolent crisis intervention processes. This allowed us to successfully handle multiple apprehensions and to de-escalate stressful encounters. Fortunately, my greatest skill and asset to the company was in my ability to complete complex fraud and internal theft investigations and to bring them to resolution. By training my teams to primarily handle the shoplifting scenarios, it allowed me to put my personal time and focus into the arena of investigations. This was very beneficial as I quickly discovered that my nervous system no longer functioned at the same level as it had before. I had to work very hard to not let it stand in my way.

Approaching and apprehending a shoplifter always has an element of unpredictability due to the unknown factor of how the shoplifter will respond. It causes a lot of stress in the body as adrenaline soars in preparation for the encounter. This adrenaline rush and stress have a direct impact on the body's nervous and physiological systems. This was particularly challenging for me with the damage my body endured due to my injuries. As is common in many SCI (spinal cord injuries), I suffer from dysesthesia, which means 'abnormal sensation.' For me, this causes my body to be hypersensitive on one half of my body and I have hypoesthesia on the other side. Hypoesthesia is total or partial loss of sensation in a part of the body. Sometimes it's accompanied by a pins-and-needles tingling. In addition to a loss of pain, temperature and touch, it is common to not feel the position of the numb part of your body. As you can imagine, not being able to fully feel your legs and feet or struggling to get them to move properly is a very dangerous thing when dealing with unpredictable people or situations. To give you a funny but true example of this, the slightest touch of something cold on my right side can make me feel like jumping through the roof. On my left side, I feel little to no sensation of pain or temperature. I was once at dinner with colleagues and was in deep conversation. I can often become animated when I talk and as I was talking with my hands, I unknowingly stuck my left pinky finger into the flame of a candle. As I was talking away, a co-worker said to me, "Uh, Mike, your finger is on fire." I looked down in shock and quickly pulled my finger out of the flame. After we realized I was not hurt, we all had a good laugh at that. Going back to the shoplifter scenarios, you can imagine how difficult it was for me to control my body and its reactions to the adrenaline surges. This affected not only how my body was physically responding but also my mind. It was crucial I was not distracted by the challenges I was having with my body. Even with all of my years of experience and the skills I had developed, I now needed to be more careful than ever in these high-stress scenarios. Surrounding myself with the right people and being even more deliberate and strategic in the training for various situations were factors essential to my/our continued success in protecting our stores, people and assets in any situation.

One key character trait I possessed throughout my career was confidence. I had strength in both verbal and nonverbal skills and the ability to appear confident even in the most stressful situations. From voice inflection to mannerisms, it is important to establish a posture of confidence, to create a presence that is not overbearing, yet one of complete control. In stressful situations I encountered daily once back at work, I discovered that controlling my right leg and nervous system was going to be very difficult. Controlling those physical responses would be crucial for my own safety and the safety of everyone around me, including the shoplifter and other guests. This included being within the confines of an enclosed office, face to face with a stranger or team member who had committed a crime. My job was to resolve the situation without becoming a liability and to ensure safety was a top priority. In full transparency, at times I occasionally felt inferior to my peers. It was a constant mental battle I had with myself. I had a mission to ensure no one else would notice this ongoing challenge I was battling through. I am human though and for the first time in my life, I found my confidence wavering. I found myself asking my reflection in the mirror, *Who am I?*

Working out and staying active during my time away from work was a huge part of being effective and prepared to do my job. This became a very important part of life for both me and Shelly. A day at the gym provided us the strengthening for not only our bodies but also our minds. It allowed us the opportunity to relieve stress and anxiety and to improve our level of confidence in both work and life. My injury was always front of mind but challenging my body physically and mentally was crucial to my journey toward improved mobility and the gaining of strength. We came to realize this would be a lifelong work in progress for us both. It became instrumental in defining who we were and how we would do life together. This consistent habit and discipline would become key in helping to define the 'new me' and who I was to become.

Once I had fully returned to work, those promises I had made to myself and to God about slowing down and putting priorities for my life in better order faded a bit into the background. I worked hard, probably harder than I had ever worked in my life. I had something to prove to others, but more importantly to myself. Even though my body sent steady reminders to slow down and be careful, I pushed right through those messages. I soon overcame many of those obstacles and started to excel at work. I started to be recognized in new ways. I began receiving nominations for awards not only in my store and district but also in my region. I was voted the district's Most Valuable Player (MVP) by my peers. I was also asked to participate in a regional assessment for a promotion. This included detailed interviews, written evaluations and self-defense, physical ability testing. I was excited yet a bit apprehensive. I would be placed under a microscope during the intense assessment process. Once again, I found myself questioning if I would be able to handle the physical aspects of my job at a new level. In the back of my mind, I was concerned that I would be perceived as weak or unable to perform the physical aspects of the job. My mind worked overtime telling me lies as to why I was not good enough. With the strong support of my supervisor and Shelly's ongoing support and inspiration, I decided to see how well I really could perform. It was a long two days for the assessment process, but it was an enlightening trip in multiple ways.

Twelve candidates from across the region were invited and each person was a standout in their respective districts. We went through multiple intense interviews and role-playing scenarios. Each of us was evaluated and scored by a team of high-level leaders from throughout our region. I must admit it was a demanding process. I had a tough time controlling my right side, and my nerve and muscle damage was one of the most challenging parts of the process for me. Even though I was confident in my level of knowledge and skill displayed throughout the process, I felt like the limitations I had from my injury were blatant and at the forefront of everyone's mind. I just knew these issues must have been a topic of conversation behind the scenes. I returned home and waited to hear from my supervisor. I was nervous, but overall, regardless of my limitations, I felt like I did well. When my supervisor came to my store to recap my assessment, he led in with the words you never want to hear, "Do you want the good news or bad news?" It was typical for him to play around, so I told him to just let me have it. The bad news was, at that time there were no open positions in the region to promote into. The good news was, out of the twelve candidates at the assessment, I scored number one and did extremely well. Holy cow! I was shocked. I was enthused for many reasons and deep down inside, I was confident in my abilities and proud of my results. This experience taught me a valuable lesson, not to listen to the lies that we tell ourselves in our own minds. Even with the many physical concerns I had to maneuver around, overcoming obstacles was (and is) just part of the journey. When you make it around those obstacles, it can be a sign you are on the right path. This sure did not mean that life was easy, but it was another indication that any setback can be turned into a comeback.

With no district team leader positions available in our region, I was asked to take on greater responsibilities to assist my boss in running the stores in our district and in training others in our field. I took on a new role as the District Inventory Resource Manager. This meant I would physically support every store in our district with their overnight inventory process. In addition to this, I was asked to take on the district responsibilities of responding to everyday security and safety concerns as a support to the stores. This was a lot to take on considering not only did I have my own store to run but now I also had to travel and be away from home. I had to work extra hard to ensure the stress and physical aspects of my responsibilities did not overwhelm me and to keep a balance with my workload. The other obvious priority was for me to continue to do my job with excellence. All things considered, I did very well and was recognized once again and asked to go to HQ for additional interviews and assessments. By this time, I had made a name for myself and I had proved to myself that I could perform the job at a higher level despite the added stresses and the physical limitations from my injury and seizures. Before I could even absorb it all, I was on a plane headed to our HQ in Minneapolis, Minnesota. I could feel this was my time to shine. This was going to be my time to officially advance into a district team leader position, something I had been working hard toward for years. If I did well, I could be relocated to an open position anywhere in the country. I felt ready!

The HQ interviews were far more intensive and challenging than the regional interviews I had experienced. I went through three different interview sessions, each one with three regional managers in the room, each asking questions. In addition to the interviewers, there was a tripod and camera on one side of the room and along the other side was a mirrored wall. It was a perfect setting to be observed and assessed from others outside of the room. Talk about stress! This had all of the elements of a pressure cooker. I did everything I could to keep my leg in check and to not have spasms. I was confident in my abilities and the answers I gave in each interview. On top of the interviews, there were role-playing exercises and a psychological examination to complete. When the two intensive days were over, I remember calling Shelly while in the airport and sharing a sense of relief and excitement. I felt good about my performance, and I could not wait to call my boss and discuss my perspective from the interviews. The only struggle I could think of which may have played a negative factor centered on my limp and leg spasms from my nerve and muscle damage.

Being this did not come back as a problem from the regional interviews I had participated in, I did not worry these would hold me back for the HQ interview process. What I did not realize at the time was that I had had a seizure during one of my interview sessions. After returning to my store the following week, I had a detailed conversation with my boss regarding the results from my interview process. During this discussion, he shared I had done very well in many of the aspects of the assessment process, and he was very proud of my performance. He also shared some things with me which made me realize I had had a seizure during the interviews. I had no idea this had happened. Not having discussed my medical history or seizure diagnosis with those leaders, I am sure they probably did not know what they were witnessing when it happened. My typical seizures are very subtle and oftentimes, people around me may not even recognize I am having one if they are not paying close attention. When I come out of my seizure state, I tend to carry on as normal with whatever I had been doing prior to having the seizure. In an interview session, there definitely would have been questions regarding my odd behavior and others would have a lack of understanding as to what they were witnessing.

I am not positive whether my having a seizure played a role in the outcome from those interviews or not, but in the end, I did not receive that promotion. Yes, I was disappointed. Yet, that experience also taught me a valuable lesson. I would not truly appreciate this lesson or the true value of it for years to come. But similar to so many tough moments I had already lived in my life, I would once again realize everything happens for a reason. Years later, things would make more sense to me. But for now, Shelly and I were part of two amazing teams and we each were in beautiful stores on the coast of North Carolina. It was a dream for this young couple from Michigan to be living minutes away from the ocean and for both of us to be successful executive leaders for a great company. And just maybe not receiving that promotion was part of a greater plan. It could have been another subtle reminder from our Creator that this was not the path He wanted me on. We like to believe He saw Shelly and I *BECOMING* the people He created us to be by doing something different from the plans we currently had for ourselves. For now, we would continue to do our best and strive for the greatest level of excellence we could achieve in our daily responsibilities and performance. I continued to work in the store I was in, which was an hour's commute from where we lived. I respected the team I worked with, we had many friends in our stores and I excelled at what I did. My drive to work was not bad, even though, on occasion I had to travel to stores throughout the district and often to the district office in Charleston, South Carolina. My time spent commuting on the road would once again present a challenge for me.

FIFTEEN

TRAGEDY OR TRIUMPH

*Trust in the Lord with all your heart; do not depend on
your own understanding. Seek his will in all you do, and
he will show you which path to take.*

Proverbs 3:5–6

The last time I was behind the wheel of a car was one which, once
again, changed the trajectory of my life. I had to travel to the district office
for my job for a two-day regional meeting in Charleston. For that trip, I
had rented a vehicle to make the long drive and to save mileage on my
own personal car. That weekend was a certification training class on nonviolent crisis intervention, and my peers and I were tested on our physical
ability to perform various techniques required for our positions. It was a
very stressful experience, but I really enjoyed that part of my training. Even
with some of my limitations, I felt confident and was eager to participate.

During the second day of the meeting and testing, I had a seizure. While we were in small groups of three to four people, we were doing role-playing scenarios utilizing the proper techniques needed to apprehend shoplifters. One minute we were in the midst of executing these techniques with one another and the next thing I remember is being surrounded by people who were asking me if I was alright. A short break was called while the leaders worked to assess my condition and to ensure I was ok and did not need further medical assistance. Someone had gotten me water and I sat down for a bit until I felt like I was back to 'normal.' I was very embarrassed this happened in such a public and open forum, not only with my peers but also with the regional leaders who were present. So naturally I did what I had always done—I pretended it did not happen and I got back to work as if nothing at all had happened. We continued our meeting to the conclusion without further incident. That was not the first time a few others had seen me have a seizure, so they knew a bit of what to expect. Most often, my complex partial seizures could easily be mistaken for fatigue or maybe a lack of proper nutrition. I was grateful to have completed the meeting and to have received my recertification necessary to continue in my position. I felt prepared and ready to take the information and techniques I had learned back to my team and to start training them.

Once the meeting had ended later that afternoon, I had gotten into the car and started on my 3.5-hour drive home. During the drive, I remember stopping somewhere on the way out of Myrtle Beach for something to eat. I thought it was a Burger King, but I could not figure out exactly where that would have been on the route I had taken. What I do remember next is, as I was driving over the bridge leading into downtown Wilmington, I looked over and realized the side mirror on my car door was hanging by a thread. *What the heck!* I thought to myself. As soon as I crossed that bridge, I drove into a parking lot of a closed business and got out to check out the car. I could not believe what I was seeing. The car had a lot of damage on the hood, driver's-side door and even the roof. It looked as if I had driven through brush, maybe a briar patch, a fence or something. I had no idea what had happened, but here I was, an hour from our house, dazed and confused. I sat back with a sick feeling in my stomach, worried that something terrible had happened. I just did not know what or where. I was startled, very upset and extremely shaken with my situation. Obviously I had had another seizure, but where? When? And had anyone else been involved in the accident? As I sat there trying hard to remember exactly what had happened, I vaguely recalled a man knocking on my window asking me if I was ok. I seem to remember just looking at him, nodding my head and then driving off as if nothing had happened. But where had this taken place? The good news was I was not hurt and although the vehicle was damaged, it was still drivable. It was about 8:30 p.m. and I knew I could not get back on the road. I called Shelly right away to let her know what had happened.

Shelly was out of town, training for an exciting new position she had just been promoted into. This was a big promotion and one which we were both very excited about. Not only was she out of town training for this new position but we were also in the process of trying to find a new home and preparing to move from our current home. Needless to say, we had a lot going on at the time! When she answered my call, I had to share the disturbing news with her about another accident I had been in. Thankfully, this time I was not hurt, and as far as I knew, no one else had been involved in the accident either. She was immediately alarmed and told me to stay right where I was, not to get back on the road and she was on the way to me. It would take her about two hours to get there, so I settled back to wait for her in the well-lit parking lot I had stopped in. While waiting, I called the NC State Police and shared with them what had happened. I could not give them much detail, as I just could not recall it, but I did share with them the general area where I believed the accident could have happened and the approximate time of night it happened. I had the direct contact and phone number for an officer on duty that night and told him that as soon as Shelly arrived, we would make our way back toward Myrtle Beach to try and determine where my accident had occurred. I was very grateful that no other accidents or injuries had been reported from any hit-and-run accidents that evening in the area in question.

When Shelly arrived, we had a very emotional reunion. It was surreal going through another accident situation late at night, on my way home from work. We were both so grateful I was not hurt, and we were very concerned at the potential damage I may have caused with whatever it was I had hit. Once we were calm and collected, we got back in the damaged rental car and headed back toward Myrtle Beach. As Shelly drove, I called the State Trooper to let him know where we were, and we set up a meeting location in Brunswick County. We searched the roadside as we drove, keenly looking for signs of an accident. We did not see any signs at all as we drove all the way back, nearly to the outside of Myrtle Beach. When we met the officer, he too had been searching for a potential accident scene and had not been able to find one. He looked at the car, did an interview with me and took a report of the accident. Because we were unable to find the actual location of the accident, we eventually were free to go and return home. We returned to the empty parking lot in Wilmington and left the rental car there for the rest of the night. We drove home in Shelly's car and returned the following day with a friend to retrieve the rental car. That evening was the last time I have been behind the wheel, driving a car. It was the beginning of June 2006. And my life would once again take a major detour in the plans I had set for myself.

On the drive home that night, Shelly and I had some very tough and hard conversations about my health, the various seizure scenarios I had been dealing with and what that meant for my/our future. We talked well into the wee hours of the morning. The number one concern was for not only my safety but also the safety of others on the road. Shelly said it well when she said I was unintentionally playing 'Russian Roulette' every time I got behind the wheel. It just was not worth taking that risk any longer and I was not willing to put others at risk. The next day I had a lot to do. Not only did we need to return the rental car and explain what had happened to them, but I also had many calls to make, including to my boss and our human resources division. I could no longer ignore the impact my seizures were having on my own health and safety, as well as the potential impact I could have on others. Because my position at work included not only an hour's commute one way to work but also much driving to various meetings, training events and support to other stores, I had to make a tough decision. I made the decision to take myself off the road and to not drive again until we found an answer to my seizure disorder. The only answer which would be acceptable in order to drive again would require a treatment which would 'cure' my seizures and allow me to have 100% control of them. I took a medical leave of absence from work, and we got busy scheduling doctor appointments and doing research for a new neurologist. A massive amount of testing and new doctors' appointments were on the horizon for me, including those at the neurology department at Duke University. As if we did not already have a lot on our plates with Shelly taking on a new position, trying to sell our home and a move to a new city/state, we were also now taking on the new challenges of me no longer driving and having to juggle the many different doctor appointments into the schedule. We did not know how we were going to effectively handle the challenges we were now facing, but somehow, we knew together we would find our way.

We have a core belief that all things happen for a reason and there is a lesson or silver lining in each, no matter how difficult it is going through it. As difficult a situation as it was for me to make the decision to put my career on hold, we would once again find much meaning and new direction out of that scenario. One positive thing about my being on a leave of absence and now home from work was it allowed me to handle the coordinating and a lot of the preparing and packing of our house for our upcoming move. This allowed Shelly to have more focus as she stepped into her new position. She completed her training and reported to her new store on July 3, 2006. She was living in a furnished rental apartment until we found a new house to live in and were able to complete our move. We did a bit of long-distance living for a few months with Shelly making many trips home to me. We had to plan strategically for those times she was away to ensure I had the groceries and other needs I might have taken care of for the time she would be out of town. I rotated between being at our house and staying with her in Myrtle Beach so that not only could she work but also, we could continue our house-hunting together. It took over four months for us to find a house we felt we could call home. By now, her workload was extremely high, as her store was in the middle of one of the busiest times of year in Myrtle Beach, the summer tourist season. She would come to refer to that time of year as 'Disney World on steroids.' Not only was the store extremely busy but it also came with many new challenges, her being new in her position and having an entirely new team of people working for her. To say her plate was full is an understatement. But she was loving her new store and team, and we were both grateful for the opportunity this move provided for us. We were very happy and excited for our future, even though I was still trying to figure out my next move.

After weeks and months of various doctor visits, tests and trips to Duke University, we still did not have an answer to resolving my seizures. Unfortunately, for most people who suffer from epilepsy, there is no cure. The most critical question we were now faced with was, was it safe for me to continue to drive? Was putting myself and the lives of others in jeopardy worth my staying in a career and with a company I loved? There were so many things to consider, but deep down inside, I knew the answer. I would never want to put someone else's life in danger. I, more than anyone else, knew the impact and devastation that a traumatic car accident could cause to someone's life. Until this point, I had spent my entire adult life under the care of a neurologist and with the approval to drive as long as I was on the proper medication. Yet, some minor incidents I had had with seizures and this last accident on my drive home from Charleston had proved to me it was time to surrender my license. I was once again losing a source of independence and mobility. I had previously been on a mission to 'lose my wheels' when in the hospital, confined to a wheelchair. But I never thought I would be losing *these wheels*. The wheels of my car, which did not only help to provide my income and profession, but which were also deeply linked to my sense of self and significance in the world. This loss of independence rocked me. It hit me at the core and left me reeling, unsure of who I was and what my purpose in this world was. It critically challenged my ability to contribute financially to our household. My entire identity as a security professional was in jeopardy. This had been my mission and my focus for what I wanted to do in this life. Returning to my team and position at work had been a driving factor and support in helping me through all the pain and struggle, the hard work and effort in getting through those days, weeks and months of rehabilitation after my accident. How could I walk away from my career now? On top of this all, the most important part of my decision would place more pressure on Shelly's shoulders as she would become the sole provider for our household while I was at home trying to recreate myself in this new world of mine.

Like so many moments in life, the hardest experiences we go through have a way of uncovering the true strength of who we are at the core. This would be another one of those moments not only for me but for Shelly as well. We had no idea at the time the path we were about to walk down and the stage which was being set for our future. We officially moved to Myrtle Beach in September of 2006 and into our new home. That following December, I made one of the hardest decisions I ever had to make in my life. I officially resigned from my position with my company and voluntarily surrendered my license to drive. I was now faced with being tied to the four walls of our new house while Shelly spent many hours handling the demands of her store, moving from the very busy tourist season and into the back-to-school season and then straight into the holiday season. Spending so many hours apart was hard on us both. I felt alone and Shelly felt a tremendous amount of guilt spending so many hours at work. It pulled at both of us and I tried to hide from her how I was truly feeling. As she battled through the long hours demanding her attention at work, I struggled to find my way and sense of worth as I searched for new career options working from home. As we tried to settle into another 'new normal,' we both wondered together, *What have we gotten ourselves into?*

We all have challenges, trials and tribulations in our lives. Hard moments which make us question who we are and what our purpose on this earth truly is. We have those experiences which shake us to our core, make us doubt what we have thought to be true. Moments which change the trajectory of our path to the future in a split second. So many of these experiences can be dark and overwhelming, bringing us feelings of depression, fear, sorrow, anger, maybe even hatred. It is part of being human. And it is also life. How do we respond during the struggles of life? That is the magical question which makes us each unique and distinct. The answer to that question is what forms the foundation to our future. Shelly and I both believe strongly in the power of taking the darkness of trials and tribulation and turning it into the light of opportunity. Turn that darkness into the opportunity to do a greater good. To help you determine a greater purpose for your life. Take that loss and turn it into victory!

Shelly and I often think of our life experiences. Regardless of how challenging any of them have been, we strive to find the blessings in each. There is something through each one of those experiences which has brought positivity into our lives. When thinking of my spinal cord injury, I could get caught up in the *why me* negative mental state. This is a common question many people ask themselves, especially when dealing with traumatic situations. But a more important question might be *why not me?* One question has a self-limiting connotation to it and can cause people to become stuck in that state of mind. The other conjures up introspective thoughts and works to instill some accountability to a situation and some control in how one responds to it. I choose to think, *Why not me?* Looking at a situation in this way helps one to recognize my experience could happen to anyone. Why would I think I would somehow be exempt from all bad things happening? Instead, I want to focus on what I can learn from every situation, no matter how dark or difficult it is. If I can find the lesson or 'gift' in any situation, I can use that to propel me forward in a direction I want to go in. It does not mean these experiences have all been roses and sunshine. But through each, there has been some type of change within us which has produced something positive and helped create the foundation that we stand on today.

As I sat in our new house, I could only feel a sense of loss and disappointment. I was at home now, no longer driving, and Shelly was out the door every day. She was in the retail grind of the busy summer season in Myrtle Beach, crossing over with the added craziness of back-to-school shopping. Right from there, business went directly into the fall and fourth-quarter holiday season. To say that is a very hectic time for any retailer is an understatement. Running a large mass-merchant discount retailer in a busy tourist town booming from the influx of people at the beach moved the needle on the hectic scale up a few notches. I felt a part of me was missing from not being in the stores during this critical time of year, contributing to the overall profitability and safety of the stores and team. Like so many others who have experienced a career change, loss of a job or a major life-altering health crisis, I was no longer contributing financially to our household. A part of who I was had dramatically changed. I felt lost and kicked down. But I was not going to stay down. I was determined to recreate myself.

We created a new routine. I was up every day, regardless of how early the hour, making fresh coffee and a power shake for Shelly to take with her to the store. On her commute, she would call me and always say the same thing, "Hi, Honey! I hope you have a good day. I love you!" She would discuss her agenda and plans for the day. I was a good sounding board for her as she talked through projects or challenges she was dealing with. Having worked for the same company, in the same environment, offered me the ability to listen more deeply and have a greater understanding of what she was going through than if I had worked in a different industry. This gave me an additional level of support I could offer her, even in a greater way than if I had still been working myself. I found value in that. I soon found new projects to occupy my time and contribute to our household in a different way. I became a pro at washing windows, cleaning gutters and standing in the driveway with the hose, washing away the pollen. I had flashbacks of my dad doing the same thing years ago. I was doing what I had previously laughed at and thought of as those things most men do once they retire and have too much time on their hands. But these were necessary tasks to maintain the health of our home. I became accustomed to which days the men's and women's golf leagues played. I would often hear "Hello Michael" coming from someone in a golf cart driving down the fairway. I imagine I was the talk of the neighborhood. I was *that* guy, the one always on the ladder or doing projects outside. I was productive every day, but I was still missing a very important piece of my soul.

The purchase of a new Apple desktop computer was a game changer for me. I went from using a PC to a Mac. This was the equivalent of going from Target to Walmart or Coke to Pepsi. At the time, this was something which just did not happen that often. I had always been what I would affectionately call 'technologically challenged.' I had a very basic level of knowledge and skill. Having never had an Apple product, I had no idea how to maneuver through this new platform of technology. But I was determined to learn! Unknowingly, within a month I would be challenged to learn about my new computer much faster than I could have imagined. One afternoon, I was sitting at our desk working through learning some new programs. We had a storm rolling into the area and it had suddenly gotten dark and started raining. As I looked out the window, I just happened to catch a lightning bolt hit the ground across the fairway. The next thing I knew, my new desktop went black. It was completely dark and would not respond to anything I tried to do to get it going again. I could not believe it. We had spent so much money on this beautiful new desktop computer. It was supposed to lead me into my future. And now it was completely dark. As I sat there stunned and having a bit of a panic attack, I remembered something critically important. We had purchased the Apple Care plan when we bought the computer. Thank God for that! I was about to find out if Apple truly did live up to the hype about their quality products and fabulous service.

The following morning, sitting in front of my black screen, I nervously called the Apple Care number provided. Their tech support people are called 'geniuses' on the Apple website. Well, this was great because I sure needed a genius now. Almost immediately into the call, not only did I realize I was dealing with a top-notch professional, but he also immediately realized what my problem was. He politely interrupted me and said, "Mr. Warner, I know what your problem is. Your digital display board was burned out. Will you be home Wednesday?"

In the morning, just two days after the dreaded lightning strike, a van slowly drove down our street and into our driveway. A professional-looking man dressed in well-pressed khakis and a polo shirt walked to our front door carrying a large briefcase. This briefcase safely held our new digital display board which had been shipped overnight from California to Charleston. The technician had picked it up and driven nearly three hours from Charleston to arrive at my house by 11:00 a.m. Now that's what I call service! The technician entered our office, set his briefcase down and went to work. First, he laid out a cloth over our carpet. Next, he put white gloves on, carefully attached suction cups to the screen of our desktop and made a couple of adjustments. Yes, white gloves. I was amazed. He removed the screen and carefully placed it on the cloth he had lain on the floor. Within 20 minutes, he had replaced the old board with the new one and we were back in business. The desktop worked perfectly from that day on.

I realized that day the importance of quality customer service. Now, with an equipped home office, I was determined to find my new career path from home. I was venturing into uncharted territory for me, and I was feeling anxious. Security administration was what I had known and depended on as a career path. With the guilt of Shelly working so hard and now being the sole provider, I was driven to open my mind to new possibilities of what was ahead. Along the way, I began teaching myself how to use an entirely new desktop and operating system. I read everything I could find on using this new technology and I went directly to Apple's website to learn from the 'geniuses.' I decided to tap into the great resources and customer service technicians available through our Apple Care plan and I began to work directly with them. Every time I had a question, even a simple one, I called Apple Care and had a conversation with someone new each time. These 'geniuses' were so patient and helpful and would share their knowledge and expertise with me. They became virtual friends, and I turned this new opportunity into one of the best learning experiences of my life. I was becoming a geek and I liked it. I quickly discovered that I was more creative, resourceful and smarter than I had ever given myself credit for.

I started educating myself about home-based businesses and found that with an entrepreneurial mindset and an open mind, technology allowed us to harness the power of the internet making connections around the globe. I created a strategy before joining the popular social platforms and decided that while at home, I would learn as much as I could about other business models. It became obvious very quickly that working from home was an intriguing possibility. As I learned more about the power of my desktop, I started learning more about photography and software that allowed my creativity to stand out. I started making videos and books for others. As the word got out, I started receiving more phone calls, which allowed me to discover a creative side hustle. From creating graduation picture books and videos, to helping people celebrate milestone birthdays and retirement, my home office quickly became a production studio. Not only was I productive but I also started believing what Shelly and others had been telling me. I was creative and had a good eye for photography. This allowed me to once again believe in myself and helped me find a new purpose in my life. While it sure did not match my salary I had at Target, working from home taught me some very valuable lessons. And it made me realize that although money is obviously very important for each of us to live, it is not the driving force I wanted to have for my life.

SIXTEEN

IN TANDEM

Since they are no longer two but one, let no one split apart
what God has joined together.

—Matthew 19:6

The definition of 'in tandem': in partnership or conjunction; working or occurring in conjunction with each other. This seems to describe me and Shelly quite well. It is how we have built our life and our relationship together. I think this was cemented in how our relationship even came to be. We were friends for more than four years before we started dating. Although we had an instant attraction to each other from the beginning, we were both in other relationships when we met. Our paths would cross over the years as we worked together on and off at various stores over those initial years. But one thing remained steadfast during those early years and is still true today: we were good friends to start with. Relationships are

190

like partnerships. They ebb and flow, have friction at times and demand balance and flexibility in order to be successful. No successful relationship or partnership is single-minded or one-sided. In fact, the magic in the mix is the balance of all of those separate 'ingredients' simmering together to make the delicious whole. Shelly and I know a little something about balance. Literally and figuratively.

Shelly has what we like to call the 'endurance gene' from her family. Each person in her family showcases endurance in their own unique way and oftentimes it is in sports or athletics. Shelly has always had a love of the outdoors and has been active her entire life. She loves running, cycling, swimming, rollerblading, skiing, you name it. She swam competitively through high school with the 500M freestyle event her race of choice. Her love of sports and staying active continues to this day. For years, she tried to get me to ride a bike. I had no interest in it, until we moved to Myrtle Beach. One day, she talked me into going to the beach and renting beach bikes. It was a gorgeous day, and the timing was perfect as it was low tide. We rented our bikes and headed for the sand. We had a blast! It was so much fun as we pedaled down the beach laughing and scanning the ocean for signs of dolphins. We felt invincible and powerful as we rode with the wind and watched so many people just lying on their towels in the sand. *Wow were they missing out on all the fun!* we thought. I could not believe I too had been missing out on this for so many years. We rented bikes at the beach one more time and then decided we needed to buy our own. We went to a local bike shop and purchased our own beach bikes. These were not only great for the beach (obviously if they are beach bikes) but also perfect for riding in our neighborhood and on trails too. Now we were riding often, whenever we felt like it. As we got better and stronger and were

riding more and more miles, Shelly wanted to get us involved with endurance rides. She has a passion for going long and getting involved in events
which serve a greater purpose, do a greater good for others. Her previous experience running marathons with Team in Training (TNT) to raise
money for Leukemia & Lymphoma had cemented this passion of being
involved in endurance events for nonprofit organizations. Now she could
envision us doing this with cycling. There was only one problem though:
my seizures. You see, we had some mishaps while cycling in the neighborhood when I had a seizure while riding the bike. Fortunately, I did not get
hurt in these instances, as Shelly was able to quickly spot me going into a
seizure. She would notice something was wrong, then race to where I was,
jump off her bike and chase me until she could grab the seat of my bike and
pull it to a stop. Imagine that visual for a passerby! We often laugh about
some of these memories as they are quite funny in hindsight (knowing that
no one got hurt). When I go into a seizure, it is as if I freeze in the moment
(partial consciousness), in whatever I am doing at the time. In the case
of the bike, what is so interesting is I would keep my balance on the bike
while in the seizure. Envision me pedaling along and then just going into a
freeze-frame moment. I would continue in whatever direction I had been
pedaling, straight up on the bike with handlebars steady and legs in a still
position with my feet still on the pedals. It is quite bizarre to think about.
The bike would just drift along until either a) I would run into something
or b) it would run out of momentum. Luckily, this allowed Shelly to most
often be able to catch me before either of these things happened and she
could stop me and keep me safe until I completely emerged from my seizure. There was only one time she did not catch me, and we crack up about
it every time we talk about it or pass the house where it happened. We

were rounding the curve of a cul-de-sac and Shelly had gotten a bit too far in front of me. She talks to me constantly while we ride for a couple of reasons, but one of those is she knows if I am responding, I am ok. On that day, she was chattering away and up ahead of me. When she asked me a question and I did not respond, she looked back and noticed I was in a seizure. *Oh crap!* she thought. What she saw was me in complete freeze mode, heading straight for a solid brick mailbox surrounded by a flower bed. She was too far in front of me to get to me in time and could only watch as I slowly bumped up the curb into the yard. In slow motion, still frozen on the bike, I slowly fell over into the flower bed. I didn't get hurt and I was still in the seizure when she got to me. It took a few minutes for me to come out of it fully and we sat there until it was safe for me to get back on the bike again. We moved back into the street and Shelly double-checked the flower bed to ensure I had not damaged any of the flowers. Luckily, no damage was done and no harm to me. Once we knew I was ok, we got back on the bikes and hightailed it home. We laughed all the way. We were so glad no one saw me do that! How embarrassing. Having had a couple of these moments of seizures on the bike made us more acutely aware of the danger of my cycling on my own bike. We felt safe in the neighborhood or on the beach but riding on an open road or for any kind of distance was definitely out of the question. Yet we really wanted to do an endurance ride. Then Shelly came up with a brilliant idea. "What about a tandem?" she asked.

We talked about getting a tandem and Shelly felt if she rode on the front of the bike and I had a seizure, she could keep control of the bike and get us to safety until I came out of my seizure. Of course, never having ridden a tandem in my life, this was just a theory. We had no idea if it would really work. She began researching bike options online and found one we both fell in love with. It was an advanced model beyond our skill level at that point, but we wanted a bike we could grow into. We were looking ahead to a future of cycling together and doing long-distance rides. The bike she found was perfect. It was a Cannondale, and it was red and white. Perfect colors and a beautiful bike. Now we just had to figure out how to find it. We visited multiple bike shops not only in South Carolina but also North Carolina in search of it. Most bike shops do not have tandem bikes in stock as they are just not that popular. They are expensive bikes to keep on hand and they take up a lot of space to store. We were completely fine with ordering one, but we did want to test it out together before we actually bought it. Most of the shops told us we had to buy it upfront if we ordered it. And even worse? We had employees from a couple of those shops tell us the bike was too advanced for us. They told us we needed to step down and maybe buy a tandem cruiser first, not a road bike. They would not order the bike we wanted, the Cannondale. Seriously?! Obviously, we walked out of these shops never to return. No skin off our back to not give them our money. This obstacle would not stand in our way. Not only were we not deterred but we were also more determined than ever to get this bike. It became a new mission. We finally found a great bike shop in Wilmington, North Carolina, to order it for us. They even told us we could return it if it did not work out for us. Well, there was no way we were not keeping this bike once we got it. We saw it as our future! The day the bike was finally in, and we were able to pick it up, we drove up to Wilmington to get it. Shelly took it for a solo test drive out of the parking lot and jumped off it as quickly as she had gotten on it. She panicked for a minute and lost her confidence to be able to steer it. It was so much lighter than our beach bikes and she felt like she was steering a wet noodle. The bike felt like it was flowing in the wind behind her. She not only worried about her ability to control the bike but also had the added weight of responsibility of another person (me) to protect on the bike. She steadied herself for a minute, caught her breath, let her heart rate slow and then she got back on it. She rode it around for a bit and came back flushed with a huge smile on her face. "This is awesome!" she said. She regained her confidence in her own abilities and the excitement for what the bike meant for us. She couldn't wait for us to get home so we could practice with it in our own neighborhood. We loaded up the bike with the other new gear we bought to go with it and headed home. We would test our theory about my seizures and find our answer the first time out on the bike together.

Riding a tandem is not easy. You have the weight of two people on one bike and each person is trying to ride in their own, respective way. Kind of like two people living life together. To have an ability to ride a tandem successfully, you must find a balance together. Communication between both riders is critical. The stoker (the person on the back) must have trust in the captain (the person on the front) to steer correctly and maneuver the bike safely in all situations. The captain is responsible for steering, gear shifting and braking. The stoker is a second set of eyes on the back and adds power for pedaling. Both riders need to find a rhythm for pedaling. It is awkward at first to figure out how to balance yourself with the weight of another person on the bike. The captain must keep the bike steady and must rely on the stoker to keep their balance steady. The stoker must rely on the captain to steer the bike safely and steadily, but they also must read the body language of the captain. For example, they both need to lean properly if a bike is going into a turn. We often say riding a tandem can do wonders for a relationship in so many ways, improved communication being one of the best. Our first test ride on the tandem together would be a defining one. We would come to find out if our idea in finding a way around my seizures would work. We struggled through the initial experience of figuring out how to ride the tandem. We were slow and unsteady, stopping and restarting multiple times. Initially, we stayed in the cul-de-sac we live on. At first, as we approached the curve of the street, Shelly would stop the bike and we would both get off so she could walk it around the curve. She was afraid she could not cut the angle of the turn. But as we practiced, she gained confidence and soon we were rounding those curves, still upright on that bike. It was such a rush! As we began to feel steadier, we decided to take it around the neighborhood. We had only ventured about a mile before it happened. I had a seizure. The first time out! Shelly was doing her usual chatter of conversation when suddenly she felt a stronger pull on the bike. It was not quite as easy to pedal. She started asking me questions, and when I wasn't responding she knew. Darn! *Here we go*, she thought in a bit of a panic. Luckily, because the pedals are synced together, when one person pedals, both sets of pedals move. My feet stayed on the pedals as she started to slow the bike and bring it to the side of the road to stop it. Not knowing what would happen when she actually stopped the bike, she tentatively brought it to a slow stop. As soon as she could, she put her feet down in order to steady not only the bike but also me, who was frozen on the back. Interestingly enough, when the bike stopped and she put her feet down, I too put my feet down, even though I was still in the seizure. We both stood there with the bike between our legs and our hands still on the handlebars. Mine were frozen in my grip and Shelly was keeping the bike steady. She could not swing her leg off the bike because I was right behind her. She had to wait me out until I finally came out of my seizure. As I started to come around and started talking to her again, she gently instructed and guided me to get off the bike. I did as she instructed and moved back from it so she could get off as well. She gently laid the bike on the ground and came over to me. Checking me out and ensuring I was ok, she talked through what had just happened. She was shaking from nerves and adrenaline, but we were both so excited. It worked! It actually worked! She could tell immediately when I had gone into the seizure and had been able to control the bike through it all until she brought us to safety. We were so glad to have this test happen not only in the safety of our neighborhood but also on the first day! Talk about jumping into it headfirst on day one. Boom! Problem solved and we were ready to go the distance. Talk about a message from God? We definitely felt His presence with us that day.

Our first major long bike ride event was the Michigan MS 150. It was a two-day fundraising event for Multiple Sclerosis covering 150 miles of the western side of Michigan. We would ride 75 miles each day, a new personal best in distance for us both. The race started and ended at Hope College, in Holland, Michigan, on both days. The first day we travelled out and back to the north and the second day we did the same to the south. We travelled through the beautiful, scenic coastal communities along Lake Michigan in gorgeous summertime weather. This was an extra special event for a couple of reasons. One was we did it with Shelly's brother Greg, who is an experienced endurance athlete and cyclist himself. He was doing the MS 200 as he had signed up for the 100-mile distance for each day. He did this race annually and Shelly had always wanted to join him for it. We had a funny moment happen on the first day. The ride had begun, and we were a few miles into it. Shelly and I were both pedaling hard, feeling like we were going uphill. We were not, but to us flatlanders from the beach, this felt uphill for us. Greg was riding along with us, almost casually as he was turning back to talk to us and just easily cruising along. Out of the blue he said, "I can't believe you guys are here." "What do you mean?" Shelly asked. He replied, "I know you said you were going to do this race, but I really did not think you would do it. I am so surprised you actually showed up." *What?! How could he say this?* we thought. We had been training for months for this event. He completely underestimated us, something which has been a common theme in our lives. As surprised at this comment as we were, it just fueled us even more to do our best and make this weekend happen with success. Another special aspect of this event was we did it in honor of Shelly's cousin. Her cousin Sally and her family live in Holland, and Sally has MS. Sally is now in her 60s, but she has lived in a nursing home since she was 29 due to her condition with MS. It is incredible to think this amazing woman has spent her entire adult life living in a senior center. She is bedridden and cannot move around without the assistance of others and a wheelchair. Her body may have failed her, but her mind is sharp as a tack! She is a wonderful person and so interesting to talk to. The highlight of our ride and weekend was after we finished the event, all three of us (including Greg) went to visit Sally and share with her about our weekend and why we did the ride. This was something Greg had done for many years for Sally, but it was a first for us. It was also the first time I had met Sally in person. We had a wonderful visit with her and some others in the family. True to form, Greg gave Sally his medal from the ride. This was a tradition he had with her every year. It was a very special experience for us all. We would love to do this event once again someday soon.

After the MS 150 ride, we found a new goal to challenge us even further. We chose the WAM 300 Bicycle Tour for our next big event. The

WAM 300 is a three-day, 300-mile race transversing across the state of Michigan. It stands for 'Wish A Mile,' and it is the largest outdoor fundraising event for the Make-A-Wish Foundation. They call this ride 'the moving city' due to the sheer size and scope of this fully supported race. We were drawn to this race for a couple of reasons. The first reason is we were looking for a more challenging cycling event to get involved in and this one fit that agenda with the 300-mile goal. One hundred miles/day was a very auspicious goal based on our limited cycling experience both with distance and history on the bike. Another draw to this race was it is a fundraiser for the Make-A-Wish Foundation, one which is very near and dear to our hearts. We have a nephew, Dallas, who has cerebral palsy and is wheelchair bound. Dallas is one cool dude, and even though he is differently abled physically, he is cognitively very sharp. In fact, we think working for Apple HQ someday would be a great career for him. Watching Dallas develop and overcome so many challenges in his young life has been very significant for us. He was our inspiration to decide upon the WAM ride and to register to complete it. The other great factor was it is held in Michigan, near our family. It transverses the state from Traverse City and ends at the Michigan International Speedway in Brooklyn, Michigan. It took us months to train for this event. The 75 miles/day we rode in the MS 150 was the farthest we had ever cycled in one day. Shelly created a training strategy similar in concept to what she had used for training for marathons. We worked backwards from the '300 miles in three days' goal and put our plan on the calendar. Then we focused, followed the plan and put the training miles in. We were proud of ourselves with the dedication and commitment we had for the training. We put in hundreds of miles in the South Carolina heat, humidity, coastal winds and more. We were eating a vegan diet that year and put time, thought and energy into the right foods to fuel our bodies. We worked to create a diet we could replicate during the ride itself. We were powered by plants! Our communication and our relationship strengthened and became even more solid from this experience, not just in the training but also in the race itself. It was one of the hardest things we had ever done. At times, I would have a seizure while out training. There were multiple times I would have a seizure in the early miles, such as around the 20-mile mark, and Shelly would pull us to safety on the side of the road. We would wait out the seizure episode until I totally came out of it. We always had fluids and some type of salty snack I could have when needed. I would have a bit of this nutrition and then we would jump back on the bike and do another 30+ miles after the seizure. It is quite amazing I can do that, and my body and mind respond so well. Interestingly, I would always feel better after the seizure, and we would finish strong most of the time. We put so much time and planning into each training ride, trying to replicate what we envisioned we would be doing during the ride. We even slept on air mattresses and cycled for three days in a row, replicating what we would be doing on race weekend. I thought Shelly was a bit nuts when she suggested it, but it really helped us to prepare for what was to come.

The weekend of the WAM ride was one of the most amazing experiences in our lives. We had many 'firsts': cycling in the rain (true story, and it rained all three days); cycling on hills and handling much elevation; riding farther than 75 miles for the first time (and we did it three days in a row); cycling amongst a large group of other cyclists (there were over 900 cyclists participating that year); battling a seizure at the beginning of day two and then adding 84 more miles afterward; major sores and chaffing in places you don't want to know about and more. Starting day three, we were walking to our bike and a guy walking behind us said to me, "Is that a 300-mile limp?" I responded with "No, it's a spinal cord, 1,500 lb. cow limp." That sure was a good lead-in to a conversation with a stranger. We also had to deal with multiple comments from others during the weekend about the fact I was on the back of the bike and a female was the captain on the front. If only those guys who heckled us had any idea what my story was. I am quite sure none of them had been paralyzed from the neck down and were now completing this event and struggled with seizures on top of that. The final day challenged our mental fortitude to the limit. Shelly had a bit of a breakdown around mile 19 as we struggled to get to the top of a steep hill early in our ride that day. We were exhausted, our legs were like jello, we were in pain and freezing. We finally made it to the top of the hill and Shelly pulled over for a rest. She was crying and in pain from a major blister in a sensitive place. I was frustrated and wanted to keep moving and we had a 'moment.' She let out some frustration, shed a few more tears and continued to cry for the next 20+ miles. It was not until we hit the 50-mile mark and had some lunch did we start feeling like we could actually finish the ride. We were more than ready to hit that finish line. I wish you could experience what we did as we approached and entered the speedway. It was so incredible it is hard to describe. On the outside of the speedway itself, we passed the 'Silent Mile,' which is a portion of the racecourse that had remembrance stars for many children who had lost their battle with disease on this earth. It was so powerful it sucked the wind out of us and moved us to silence and tears. The magnitude of the significance of this event was powerful. It was literally hard to breathe. As we left that area, we entered the track and the energy completely changed. You could feel the excitement in the air as we started this final leg. Imagine hundreds of cyclists, many of them part of large corporate groups, riding together, laughing, cheering and celebrating the finishing mile of the weekend as we circled the racetrack. As we rounded the final curve toward the finish line, there they were, our family in the center area, looking for us and cheering wildly, signs flying in the air and smiles dominating their faces. We had no idea so many of them were going to be there to see us finish. There were so many spectators there, it was initially hard to see them. But then I heard "Michael!" in a loud shout. I looked over and there was Bob shouting and pointing at me with an incredible look of pride and happiness on his face. This was the highlight of my finish, as I had no idea he was going to be there. To have my twin brother witness me finish this incredible event is something I will never forget. It was an extremely special and memorable moment. While I was looking and waving at people, Shelly was trying her hardest to keep the bike steady so we would not crash going across that finish line. She couldn't even look at our family yet. The outpouring of emotion as we finally got off our bike and were able to connect with them was something else. Tears were flowing from everyone, and we were so happy to be done and to have them there to share the moment with us. My mom had made two very bright and creative signs for us on poster boards and put them on sticks. They were HUGE and could not be missed. We loved them! They were so perfect, and we still have them to this day. When we finished that race, we felt like we could fly. If we could bottle that feeling, we would be millionaires. The finish area was a huge party with cyclists, family, friends and Wish Kids (children who receive a wish from the Make-A-Wish Foundation) all celebrating together. Such a powerful, impactful moment and experience we will remember for the rest of our lives. I could not believe my body had just allowed me to do what we did. But looking around at all the Wish Kids, and realizing why we were there to start with, is something very hard to describe. The few short days and a little bit of pain and struggle we experienced to accomplish those 300 miles is nothing in comparison to what those kids and their families go through every day of their lives. Being amongst so many people coming together to accomplish a greater good is the elixir to life.

We have created a life designed by God and shaped by our circumstances. The way we have responded to these circumstances has directed us to the pathway we are on today. In tandem is not only a great metaphor for how we live life together; it is actually what we do. It's not always easy; sometimes it's downright scary, and often we disagree on things. But we know in the end, we will be better if we do it together. Cheesy I know, but it is truth!

SEVENTEEN

PASSION BECOMES PURPOSE

Many are the plans in a person's heart, but it is the Lord's
purpose that prevails.

—*Proverbs 19:21*

Chapter 11 began with a message challenging you to think about *what you see* in the precious moments of your life. That message is about how we look outward to the world and to others. The other side of this perspective is to ask yourself how others see you. How are you accepted in the world? Being in a hospital and rehabilitation center was a safe haven for me after I had my accident. It was a place surrounded by professionals offering care and support and where people with disabilities and altered states due to injury or illness are common. Together and in that environment, we were 'normal.' Being out in the real world is an entirely different story. I had an experience years after I was released from rehab, which illustrates what

I mean by this. It was a defining moment having personal experience and insight into what life can be like for those who are confined to a wheelchair. At the time, we were part of a nonprofit organization we had helped to create called Coastal Carolina Adaptive Sports & Recreation. This organization became the first Paralympic Sports Club in South Carolina. It was designed to help those who had sustained a devastating injury or illness causing some type of disability. The vision behind this program is to offer those with differing abilities opportunities to experience life, healing and greater independence through sports. These opportunities through sports and recreation would not only strengthen their level of independence but also improve their level of confidence and social skills in many ways. This program offered adaptive sports event options to those with differing abilities, many of whom were in wheelchairs. From basketball, field events, swimming, powerlifting and surfing, we did it all. Our group was hosting a booth one year at a festival to draw additional exposure and fundraising for our program. We had with us one of our adaptive wheelchairs which was designed and used to play basketball. Many people were at this festival, but not enough were stopping by our booth. We decided to take turns and get into that wheelchair, out in front of the booth, hoping to capture the attention of passersby. The shocking truth was the opposite happened. Before this, as people had passed by, even if they did not stop at our tent, they at least looked our way and greeted us. Shelly got into the chair first and noticed a different response in people right away. It was quite shocking and honestly upsetting. She then wanted me to get in the chair to see if I would have the same response. It was my turn to sit in that chair and it was a strange and surreal moment. This could have been my reality. Having once been looking at the very real possibility of being in a wheelchair for life, I was very uncomfortable getting back into one for any reason. But this was important. It offered us an extra element to showcase to people what our program was all about and why we were there. As I sat in that wheelchair, trying to draw attention to our booth, I noticed people were not looking our way at all. They tried to go around me without even looking. As if I wasn't even there. I felt invisible. This gave me a glance into the lives of so many who must depend on a wheelchair for their daily movement. Not only do they move around differently than most and struggle with all the challenges which that brings, but they also must face darker realities each day. Being made to feel invisible. This shocking realization broke our hearts. It also had a profound impact on us and how we see others in the world. To really see people. For whom they are. To see beyond the package they are in. It is incredible how a simple moment of eye contact, a quick smile or hello can validate a person, even when coming from a stranger. It makes us wonder what causes this reaction in people to be indifferent. Is it fear because they are uncomfortable connecting with someone who looks differently than they do? Are they uncomfortable about how to approach an individual who has obvious challenges because they don't know what to say or what questions to ask? These questions and more added a new driving element for our mission in life—to try and break down the barriers which might keep people from connecting with those who are different than they are. And there is something for every one of us to think of. You never know who that person in that wheelchair is or even when that person could be you or someone you love.

For most people, facing a critical injury or experience in life can make them view life through a different lens. The fragility of life becomes much clearer and more powerful to your senses. That feeling of invincibility we so often have in youth fades. You realize you do not have complete control of your own destiny, no matter how much you think you do. There are no guarantees for any of us. If you truly desire something, have ideas of something important you want to do in the future or 'someday' when the timing is right, you may want to revisit those thoughts and passions and start working on making that 'someday' sooner than later. God has gifted each of us with unique strengths, characteristics and talents. He has gifted them to us not for us to hold onto them for ourselves but so that we could share them with the world. Those things which you feel passionate about, get your heart racing when you think of them or maybe even come so easily to you you don't think twice about them. That which comes to you so easily you could give it away for free may be the very thing others are searching for and/or need in their own lives. We feel fortunate to have gone through the adversity we have had in our lives because it has directed our path in a way we probably would not have taken had we not been through the trials we have had. Not only had I faced the possibility of being paralyzed for life, but I also had my career choices and dreams altered due to my medical condition of epilepsy. Having gone through so much of this with me, this has had a profound impact on Shelly as well. It affected her life as much as it affected mine. In addition, her brother's son Dallas was born with cerebral palsy. He is very special and very important to us. We have watched with amazement as he has grown and tackled his own obstacles with grit, determination, strength and an incredible outlook on life. His body may be challenged, but his mind and his heart are stronger than most. He has an incredible spirit with a smile and laugh which could bring world peace. Shelly and I have always had a passion to help others. Our personal experiences would come to shape how we would put forth our efforts to follow that passion. With my physical challenges and the inspiration of Dallas, we sought out a program in which we could play a more instrumental role in the lives of those with different abilities. Shelly had a background in endurance sports and training. She also had previously been involved in an organization, Team in Training, which uses endurance sports to fundraise and raise awareness for the Leukemia & Lymphoma Society. This organization is near and dear to her heart, and we discuss it in more detail in the next chapter. But that experience had had a profound impact on her life. When she discovered Team, she had never been a runner, but the mission of the organization captured her heart. She was hooked the moment she saw an advertisement for it and jumped in with both feet. This program helped her complete her first ever running event—a marathon. It also cemented the significance of being involved with an endurance training program and organization which has the goal of serving others. That program blended two passions Shelly had in her life, being involved with sports and athletics and striving to make a greater impact in the lives of others. We would soon find out that these experiences were leading us toward the next adventure of our journey together, one which would fulfill us both in a significant way.

After moving to South Carolina, Shelly had been loosely searching for years for a program like Team in Training which she could get involved in. She was extremely busy with the demands of her job, but she also was missing something very critical in her life. That light which lit her passion had started to dim in the daily grind of retail. She wanted to be involved with a community program or organization where she felt like she was doing a greater good for others. She had loved the experiences she had had with Team in Training and the friendships she had made. She was searching for something like it in our area. There was not a (TNT) chapter in our area of South Carolina, so she started looking for more options. There was a similar program she was familiar with which also utilized endurance events, primarily running, on a mission of inclusion and education for those with differing abilities. It paired able-bodied athletes with those with disabilities in racing events. Many with disabilities would normally not be able to participate in such events without the assistance of able-bodied athletes and specialized equipment to help them get from the start line to the finish line. There was not a chapter from this group in our area or even state. After making a major career change and with more time on her hands, Shelly started digging deeper to fulfill this passion in her heart. She felt strongly about the mission of inclusion, and she also felt it was too important for the people of South Carolina not to have access to such a program. We discussed it together and decided we needed to do something similar in South Carolina. After searching for any similar programs in neighboring states throughout the southeast, she discovered an amazing one called Ainsley's Angels of America (AAA). This chapter was less than two hours from our home. Shelly contacted the AAA group in North Carolina to pursue our interests in bringing it to South Carolina. Within hours of sending that first email, we were speaking with the local leader of AAA in North Carolina, Michelle Kendall Smith. Then later that same evening, we were speaking directly to the President of Ainsley's Angels. We were hooked. The President of AAA is actually Ainsley's father, Kim Rooster Rossiter. We were immediately captured by the essence of Ainsley's story and how AAA had gotten started. We were also impressed by the professionalism and authenticity of the leaders and people in this organization. The mission and vision of Ainsley's Angels of America captured our hearts, and we could not wait to get started. Holy Cow! Ainsley's Angels in South Carolina was born within 24 hours, and we were leading the way.

Being a part of Ainsley's Angels of America is so much more than running or racing. It is about family, friends, relationships and life. Having the opportunity to share in the lives of such incredible people is truly a gift from God. We are so blessed and honored to be able to serve in such a way and to have met some of the most incredible and strong people we have ever crossed paths with. To give you an idea, Ainsley's Angels of America is a 501(c)(3) nonprofit organization made almost entirely of volunteers. Our organization, or the AAA family as we like to call it, is a family of angels over 30,000 strong. As of the writing of this book, we currently have 68 ambassadorships (or locations) in 33 states. How does an organization of this size and magnitude exist with all volunteers? It can only be explained by the level of love not only for Ainsley and the Rossiter family but also for all our angel families. Sharing love and a commitment to something greater than yourself is very good and powerful indeed. And we are touched by Angels! The gifts we receive by witnessing the joy of racing and inclusion with our angels far outweigh the work and effort to make it happen. I am sure you will hear this same message from anyone at any level in our AAA family: angel-riders, angel-runners, guardian angels and any of our leaders. We are, each of us, driven by the mission. We felt strongly we had found a new 'home' and family of people to which we could take our skills, passion and love for others and accomplish something pretty amazing. We had no idea how right we would be and how much this organization would impact our hearts and our lives. We have a passion. And we have found the perfect family of people to give that passion purpose.

EIGHTEEN

WHERE THE MAGIC HAPPENS

But those who trust in the Lord will find new strength.
They will soar high on wings like eagles. They will run and
not grow weary. They will walk and not faint.

—Isaiah 40:31

The finish line. Often perceived as the end, the finish line is the place where the true celebration begins. It is the place where the months of training, the blood sweat and tears that were shed finally pay off. It is a place filled with inspiration, determination, emotion and resilience. It is also where the real stories are told. It is simply the place where the magic happens. For years I would be mistaken as a finisher. My awkward gait made it appear that I had just completed a race. Countless people would congratulate me and ask me, "How was your run?" I found this to be quite entertaining and encouraging at the same time, especially while limping in pain through airports after a long weekend from a race I didn't even run. Because of my injury, I had what appeared to be 'the 26.2-mile limp.' Shelly did not find the attention I received amusing, as she was the one who had completed the races but not many seemed to be asking her if she had completed the race. The countless events we attended were the result of her passion to do more and be more, the hours she spent training and her determination to complete races. My road to the finish line would take a very different path. One which I would not change for the world. My day, my pace, my race would be an accumulation of years of watching Shelly from the sidelines, being inspired by her and countless other athletes, each with their own incredible stories. Without them, the thought of ever becoming a participant would have stayed just a dream.

It all began with that day on the beach. We had returned to the place where we had fallen in love with North Carolina and had begun to dream of a future together. Still fighting equilibrium issues and making my already unsteady legs feel even more tenuous, we began to walk through the sand toward the pier. The waves were mellow and rhythmic, the full sun striking against gorgeous blue skies. It was a perfect day. On that day, as I thought back to all we had already endured together, I was filled with gratitude and overwhelmed with love. My heart raced with anticipation as I was about to make one dream come true. With excitement coursing through my veins, I stopped and turned Shelly toward me. Doing what I had always planned on doing from the moment we had decided to move to North Carolina, I gingerly bent down on one knee and pulled the ring from my pocket. Shelly gasped and started crying as she realized what I was doing. In my hand was the one-of-a-kind ring I had specially made just for her. She immediately rushed out a *Yes!* a second time in answer to my question to be my bride. She was overjoyed with happiness and excitement at having a ring designed and specially made just for her (not the borrowed one from my grandmother). She was stunned I had secretly been able to have a ring created for her without her knowing about it. The most important part of my future was having Shelly in it and for us to go together through whatever life would throw our way. Unbeknownst to us at the time, my proposal and the start of planning for our wedding would open the door for running and racing to become a significant part of our lives.

Time moved quickly through the year and into the following spring. As our wedding date neared, Shelly started a walking routine to get into better shape for the big day. One day while out walking, she began thinking to herself something was missing in her life. Even though we had a full life together, she was excited for our upcoming wedding and was challenged in her job, she still had a nagging feeling there was more she should be doing. She not only wanted to get healthier and back to her passions of fitness and sport but also wanted to get involved with a nonprofit. To do a greater good for others. Upon returning home from her walk, she grabbed the mail and saw an advertisement for TNT, a nonprofit fundraising group that uses endurance sport events to raise money for the Leukemia & Lymphoma Society. What a God moment this was! This was the answer to her desire to get involved with a nonprofit. One of her best friends in high school, Jill, had been diagnosed with leukemia when they were in the tenth grade, and it had a profound impact on her. Not only did TNT have a powerful mission which was very personal to Shelly, but it also had the element of endurance sports to carry out that mission. This was her answer, and she was ready to go to a meeting to see what it was all about. At least she could become a volunteer in some way. She thought to herself, *I might not be able to run a marathon, but I can at least work at a water station or help organize in some way.* That evening she researched the organization and made her plans to go to the first meeting. The closest chapter for this organization was two hours from where we lived, but she was still motivated to go to that meeting. After attending that first meeting and seeing how many different people were represented in the group of those who had already completed a marathon with TNT, she changed her mind on how she would volunteer. She thought to herself, *If all these people can do it, why can't I?* Never having run any type of racing event prior to this meeting, Shelly made a commitment that night. She would join TNT as a participant and in a few months, she would start training for a marathon. It was obvious from that moment she was on a mission. Like her work ethic, I knew nothing would stop her determination. It was amazing to watch her training for something she had never done before and to do it during the busy fourth quarter while working in discount retail. Those grueling and long 12-to-17-hour workdays did not stop her from her training goals. She had her memories of Jill and the battle Jill had fought with cancer to power her through the most difficult days.

The second weekend in January 1998 came upon us very quickly. As part of the Leukemia & Lymphoma Society Team in Training, we were now on our way to the Disney Rock-N-Roll Marathon. In an odd way, this would also be my first introduction into the power of the endurance sports world. As Shelly's own personal cheering team, support person and photographer, I too was on a mission. I had put a strategic plan in place regarding how to maneuver the monorail system at Disney and to navigate the racecourse to see Shelly at different points along the 26.2-mile route. I was ready to meet the challenges of my agenda for the long morning. As it turned out, I nailed it. With my camera in hand, I was able to see her at each mile-marker point, get her picture and then get back on the monorail to the next stop. It was stressful because I did not want to miss her and I had to be in the right spot at the right time. When I exited the monorail at the final destination, I quickly maneuvered the crowd with my limp and fatigued muscles and found a perfect location at the finish line. This would be a spot I would stand in for hours until she finished the race. My first problem was I had no idea when Shelly would actually finish. Maybe I should have paid more attention to her training and what her average pace per mile was. She gave me a goal she had set for an approximate finishing time, but this was her first experience at a running event, and she had really misjudged how difficult it would be. Regardless, I was now at the finish line and anxiously waiting for her to appear. With my heart pounding in anticipation, I prepared my camera for the perfect shot. I was ready and I stared off into the sea of runners approaching the finish line. With nearly 30,000 registered runners for this race, it was no easy task to find Shelly. With her short dark hair and the purple TNT racing singlet she was wearing, the same shirt that hundreds of others were wearing, the possibility of getting the perfect shot had become daunting. I spent the last three hours worrying with all the 'what if' thoughts running through my mind. What if she was hurt? What if she had finished already and I missed her? What if my camera battery doesn't last? What if someone gets in my way just when Shelly crosses the finish line? What if her training wasn't enough? What if she doesn't finish?

I knew my struggles paled in comparison to what she must have been going through. After all, she was running her first race ever, a 26.2-mile marathon. I also discovered that it was not easy to stand in one spot for hours. My body felt like it was breaking down and as I fatigued, the adrenaline depleted from my body. I knew one thing though; I was not going to miss her. My eyes started playing tricks on me as I focused on every runner coming toward the finish line. I was searching for that girl with short dark hair and wearing a purple singlet. I would have never guessed there were so many people who fit that description! I started to lose sensation in my hands and arms as I struggled to keep my camera ready in case one of the thousands of runners coming through that finish line happened to be Shelly. But I was not going to miss the moment. With other spectators around me also looking for their loved ones and bringing up small talk to pass the time, it felt like we were in a battle as each one of us fought to get one inch closer for a clearer shot. Suddenly, there she was! I snapped what seemed like 100 pictures in excitement. I was overwhelmed with emotion. I could tell she was in pain as she limped toward that finish line, but she was running. I was so happy and proud of her. Nearly an hour had passed her projected finish time, and during that time I had watched so many runners cross the finish line and then fall to the ground in various states of complete exhaustion and struggle. My mind had started to wander to worst-case scenarios. I had not known where she was and had worried she had gotten injured along the way. But she did finish and that was most important. This was one of the most unbelievable moments of our lives for so many reasons and the emotions were just beginning to pour out. As she crossed the finish line, she had to keep moving with the flow of the thousands of other runners to get her medal and to enter the finisher's area. Now with my weak legs, I had to maneuver the crowd and somehow find her. I saw her from a distance and noticed she was also frantically looking for me. When we made eye contact, we both started to cry. As we reached for each other over the fence it happened. The floodgates opened and did not stop. We both were sobbing and we each experienced a cry like no other time in our lives. I didn't know where the tears were coming from, but they poured out of us as we fell into a tight embrace. Shelly was a marathon finisher for the first time! Not knowing it at the time, this would not be her last. As we hobbled toward the monorail to take us back to our resort, all she would say was "Never again!" That sentiment would only last a few hours though. Later that evening, at the celebration party along with hundreds of other TNT people in attendance, we danced the night away with friends and she started discussing plans for the 'next one' she would do. This race was the beginning of great things to come in the world of running and racing for us both.

Not only was Shelly now a marathoner and an experienced endurance athlete but I was also an experienced spectator. In the years to come, I would learn and be very proud to call myself a spectator. It is through many more full and half-marathons where I would follow Shelly that my own strategy formed. My mission at every race was to 'Get the Shot' and I never missed one. I became resilient and a pro at finding just the right place to capture the perfect photo and moments. I also perfected my new-found photography and videography skills. Shelly has told me countless times that she believes that my surveillance and observation skills I acquired over the years in security contributed to my ability to capture that perfect emotional picture. I agree with her and found that attending races was a gift that our Creator had provided for me. The patience, resilience and determination were in me all along but were now being fine-tuned and used for something greater than myself. I found this to be especially true in 2015 at the 40th running of the Marine Corps Marathon. This race is known as the 'People's Marathon,' held at our nation's capital. This particular event was very special for so many reasons. Shelly was running the full marathon representing our nonprofit, Ainsley's Angels of America. We are a charity partner for this marathon, and we had 33 teams rolling in it that year. Our friend Patricia was also participating in the marathon and representing our ambassadorship from South Carolina. Patricia had been recovering for almost three years after being severely burned in a horrific house fire. She was lucky to be alive and to have survived that horrific day. She was stepping outside of her comfort zone to be an angel-rider, representing burn survivors. Nervous yet very excited to be a part of this incredible event, she too was ready for the race weekend experience. What a gift from God for all of us to be there together and to be able to connect with so many others in such a deep and meaningful way. We were surrounded by people who struggled through their own daily battles. Each one of them has such powerful stories of their own, which leave others in awe of their strength, grit, determination and perseverance. I was very familiar with each one of the 33 angel-riders planned to roll as I had been asked to create a video of each one of them who participated that year. The video was a surprise presentation shared to our entire Ainsley's Angels family at our team dinner the night before the marathon. There was not a dry eye in the room as the power of the pictures moved across the screen and the impact from the words of the songs I had used worked their way into our hearts as we watched and listened. It was moving, personal, loving and inspiring. It was the perfect motivation to end the evening and to prep all of those who would be running that 26.2 miles the following day. Those angels were set for their mission, and I was set for mine. I had a plan and a mission to get the best pictures I could to capture the essence of the day. I was bound and determined to get every one of those runners and riders who would be putting their all out on that racecourse the following morning, to get the shot for every one of those 33 teams of riders and runners.

What made this one of the most impactful sporting events of our lives was this was also the 100th road race for Ainsley. She is the daughter of Kim (Rooster) and Lori Rossiter. Rooster is not only the President of Ainsley's Angels but was also Ainsley's angel-runner. We already knew the weekend would be very special, but we had no idea at the time just how special it truly would be. Marathon morning started at 0330 with a sleepy yet focused and disciplined group gathering in the parking lot. We had detailed plans to convoy our vehicles as a group to our designated meeting spot on the military base. Four of us—Patricia, another friend Kurt, Shelly and I—were in one of the first vehicles to line up in the procession of cars in the hotel parking lot. We did not want to get lost on our way to the military base and miss our meet-up location prior to the race, so we made sure we were out there early. As we sat in the dark, waiting for the rest of our team to exit the hotel and load into their vehicles, we sat in hushed silence. It is hard to put into words and describe what we were witnessing. The feelings slammed into our hearts and souls as we watched families of our angels exiting the hotel in the cold and wet of the morning. Moving in silence, they walked, some solo, some together, some carrying angel-riders, some pushing and loading up wheelchairs into the back of trucks, most holding the plethora of other equipment necessary to support the daily needs of their loved ones who had various physical challenges. The attire worn by all, the branded Ainsley's Angels gear of pink and black, bound this gathering of individuals as one. There was no talking, only focus and determination. It was hard enough for us to get ourselves up, ready and out the door at that hour of the morning. What was more difficult to think of was the harsh reality and challenges these families faced with all the additional preparation they needed to do the same. We will never forget the image of the Rossiter family, one of the last to exit the hotel, as we watched them through the large windows into the hotel lobby area. Rooster led the way in front, carrying Ainsley. Precious Ainsley was dressed in her signature pink and black, with her long dark hair hanging almost to the floor in a beautiful braid. Right behind them was Ainsley's mom, Lori, ever present and focused on her daughter and carrying the gear they would need for the day. Bringing up the rear of the family were Ainsley's sister, Briley, and her brother, Kamden. There were no words needed to send the powerful message of love, commitment and reality that image represented for what this family had. That image will be forever seared into our memories and one which we often talk about. It was one of the most powerful and moving moments we have ever witnessed in our lives. It was raw, real, heart-stopping and loving. The only word uttered in our vehicle was 'wow.' One word which spoke so much truth. Once all the vehicles were loaded, we slowly made our way to the base and to our meeting location. The circle of prepped and ready racing chariots was waiting for the angel-riders. Riders loaded into the chairs as runners gathered around them with their teams. Family members, friends and support people mingled around chattering, assisted as needed and worked hard to capture the moment in pictures. From there we started our walking procession to the starting area for the marathon. This was another surreal moment. As we walked along the outside perimeter of Arlington Cemetery amongst hundreds of other runners, we were struck by the silence. So many people walked along in silence or hushed whispers, taking in the moment of what we were all a part of and witnessing. Surrounding us were people who had been through their own personal battles we would never know the depth of. To our right were the endless and precise rows of white crosses, signifying the depth and loss of life of those who fought for our freedom, our freedom to be present and participate in a morning such as this. We tried to take this all in as we walked in the quiet. Early morning mist, rising from the sacred ground of Arlington National Cemetery and through the trees, spoke volumes. It surrounded us in a hug of cool wetness and had us absorbed in blessings and gratitude for the heroes who sacrificed so much for our freedom as well as those heroes who surrounded us on this walk.

Our angel teams would be starting at the front of the field of runners to begin the marathon. They would start just behind the many wounded warriors who would lead the way for all. After our teams had finally made it to their starting area, I made my move. It was a new landscape for me, but I had to find the perfect spot to get those priceless pictures. As I walked away from the start, thousands of runners were still making their way toward me and to their own starting corrals. Soon I came to a barricade with a proud and stocky marine positioned for crowd control. After a friendly yet brief conversation with this young marine, he looked in both directions and slid the barrier aside allowing me to enter the area. Maybe it was the open and friendly way I carried myself, or my Ainsley's Angels gear that I was proudly wearing, but the first part of my plan was in motion. The good news was, I was in! Waiting for the marathon to start, I found myself in the first of many perfect spots I would discover that day. After a beautiful and moving rendition of our national anthem, followed by a prayer from the Marine Chaplin and then paratroopers dropping in, waving huge American flags from their backpacks, I was about to have a moment of my own. As I stood there intently, waiting for the race to begin and to be led by our AAA racing teams, I had not realized I was standing so near the starting 'gun.' It was not quite a gun. It was a cannon. A real cannon! Who would have known the race would start with a cannon? Needless to say, I was startled to attention. But the thrill and exhilaration of witnessing the incredible moment had just been taken up a notch with that cannon. Standing on the side of a hill along the interstate, witnessing our angel teams, other challenged athletes, wounded warriors and the nearly 40,000 runners starting their journey was awe-inspiring. What a magnificent start to the day! Now it was time to make my move to the finish line area and secure the perfect location to capture every team approaching the final goal—the Iwo Jima Memorial.

After a couple of quick stops along the way, I arrived at my next destination. I secured a perfect spot. I landed on the side of the race route, right along a fence which held spectators back. This was a narrow part of the final leg of the race. It was at the top of the last hill our teams would climb before making a turn to the finish line with the Iwo Jima Memorial in their sights. This spot was perfect, as I could see each team as they began their trek up from the base of the hill. I stood pressed up against that fence and pinned in by other spectators. For six hours I did not move. I caught each one of our teams as they approached victory. My location allowed me to capture the pain, grit, determination and joy of each athlete as they turned that last corner. One by one they climbed and conquered this course. Many approached with smiles on their faces, others with expressions of pain and exhaustion. But all had energy and excitement, hands in the air and a focus to race across that finish line with honor. When our last team finished, I could hardly feel my legs. But I felt amazingly accomplished. It was now time to make my way to our charity partner VIP tent and to find Shelly, Patricia, Kurt and others. It was time for celebration! I could not have been more proud and I could not wait to return to South Carolina to analyze my pictures and the videos I had taken. In my mind, I was already forming the vision of the recap video I would create. I knew no one else had captured all that I had been able to capture. Our angel families would love and cherish what I had planned for them. I loved being the 'behind the scenes guy,' as this always made me feel like a part of the team. Being a guardian angel on this day gave me the opportunity to not only capture priceless moments but also create something special, which would live on long after the race weekend. It would become a keepsake for years to come. On this day, being motivated and inspired by every one of our rider athletes at the Marine Corps Marathon was very special. The smiles from our angel-rider athletes, along with those of our angel-runners who lend their legs so our riders can experience the thrill of a race, are priceless. The 40th running of the MCM will be forever etched in my brain as one of the greatest experiences of my life.

This story is just one of many I have experienced over the years with Shelly and Ainsley's Angels, as well as with TNT. Along the way, I discovered a lot about myself while watching, cheering and capturing precious moments in pictures and videos. I felt a sense of accomplishment after every event I attended and at the same time I learned so much about the human spirit. What I have witnessed at countless finish lines has been magical. I have often said that everyone needs to experience it. It is one place where you can experience so much beyond ourselves. The athleticism, grueling determination, commitment, dedication, tears, joy, emotions and love are all encompassed with cheering spectators, music and the sound of the announcer calling out every finisher's name. The finish line is one of the most diverse, inspiring and emotional places where inclusion and acceptance are all as much a part of the atmosphere as are the medals being handed out. It is where the magic happens.

NINETEEN

FAITH TO THE FINISH LINE

*Each time he said, "My grace is all you need. My power
works best in weakness." So now I am glad to boast about
my weaknesses, so that the power of Christ can work
through me.*

—2 Corinthians 12:9

A 1% chance. That is what the doctors gave me after my accident. This was not an encouraging number. But as you have already learned, I decided early on my reality was not going to be defined by what others thought. I have purposely chosen my reality for my life to be about optimism and having a positive mindset through all situations.

Inspired by countless unsung heroes along the way, Shelly and I have discovered that our mission in life is to inspire others by taking action and leading by example. Along the way we have stayed passionate about our well-being and have been driven to be better today than we were yesterday. The message from the onset of our journey has been crystal clear to us. Keep moving forward and work to make improvements while also working to help others do the same. Over the years we have discovered that to be an athlete is defined by not only physical ability but also a combination of physical and mental preparedness. The book, *The Champion's Comeback*, written by author Jim Afremow, PhD, digs deep into the minds of athletes and explains how athletes think, train and thrive. It outlines how champions continue to persevere despite losses, injuries and other personal and professional setbacks. My mind has always been my secret weapon. This book has shown me the true power of my mindset and how it has affected the outcomes of so many situations in my life. Keeping your mind sharp is critical in moving forward. Shelly and I are a great team and we have discovered how to live life in a greater way, together. The freedom discovered and the barriers we literally rode through on our tandem together not only impacted us literally and physically but also metaphorically. Our experiences on that bike have helped affirm for us what is possible if we stay open-minded, stick together and push past our fears. A slogan we have hanging on a plaque in our kitchen confirms this thought process. It states: 'Never, Never, Never Give Up!' Holding this belief blows the doors of potential opportunities ahead wide open! Our adaptive approach has made us feel alive and inspired. It has allowed me to discover that I am strong, and I am an athlete regardless of my disabilities. One main goal I have always had has been to turn a disability into an ability to live an active and healthy life. This does not mean I ignore the fact I have a spinal cord injury and epilepsy. Instead, despite these limiting abilities, it gives me more power in my drive each day to become a better version of myself.

One day, our pastor in church made a statement which resonated with us both and has become a common mantra for us. 'Do what you can, use what you have' has become part of our lifestyle approach. I have come to realize I am capable of far more than I had ever thought was possible. If I had not had the courage to try and to start, I can't imagine where I would be today.

But what about running? This thought had always managed to elude me despite Shelly's ongoing encouragement. She would continuously stress that with the right training and preparation, someday I would run. I may look a little different, I might be slower than most and need adjustments along the way, but my mindset is also stronger than most. *What about running? Was it possible for me to do?* This seemed to be a key unanswered question I would grapple with for years.

My running journey did eventually begin, but it did not start off on the right foot. Literally, it was my weak right foot that got the best of me. We were at a health conference with hundreds of people and listening to a guest speaker. Abruptly, the speaker said, "Your row is your team!" He then passed around a piece of paper with a list of items each team had to find in a scavenger hunt race around the hotel property. Keep in mind, my body can be like a bad internet connection. Sometimes it works, other times not so well or it takes a long time to 'boot up.' But the countdown began and the race was on. I was out of my seat as quickly as everyone else and I was trying my best to keep up, hobbling along and chasing my team. Motivated by peer pressure, I tried to run and control my right side the best I could until I tripped in the hotel lobby. Feeling like I was in slow motion, I felt myself fly for a moment before going down in front of a busy check-in desk area. As I tripped, I felt myself fly through the air and then I landed on my face. Shelly was nowhere near me as our group had split into two different groups in an effort to have a better outcome and win the scavenger hunt. Immediately I was surrounded by many different people trying to assist me as they checked to see if I was ok. Unfortunately, I had landed on my face, chipped a front tooth, bit my lip and was now lying in a pool of blood. Someone called 911 and the good people around me stayed with me and worked to keep me still and calm. Meanwhile, Shelly and her group had already returned to the meeting room, and she was trying to figure out what was taking us so long. She later told me that when her phone rang and she saw my name and number flash across the screen, she answered it laughing and asking where we were and what was taking us so long. As soon as she heard a female's voice asking if she was Shelly, she started running back out of the room and toward the escalator as she spoke to the woman to get details on what was happening. She took off so fast and without thinking that she actually ran up the downward moving escalator loaded with people. She pushed past them in a panic, not even caring that she probably looked like a crazy lady. As she ascended to the top of the escalator and toward the lobby area, still speaking to a stranger, she noticed a large group of people surrounding something in the middle of the floor. EMS personnel had just arrived on the scene, and they were making their way through the group of people while the lights from their fire truck and ambulance flashed in the windows. As Shelly approached her heart dropped as she could see part of my body through the throng of legs surrounding me and she noticed the blood on the floor. As she pushed through the crowd and made her way down to the floor near me, I could hear her voice and immediately I felt more at ease that she was there. I was so worried about her and what she was probably feeling as she witnessed the chaotic scene. The EMS team was working hard to assess my injuries and they were trying to get me to sit up. After answering a few quick questions from the first responders, Shelly clarified with them that I was well enough to be transported to an emergency room or doctor's care in our own vehicle. After ensuring I was in good hands with the EMS team, she took off to get her purse and raced to the parking structure to get our jeep while they worked to bandage up my head and mouth. Luckily, one of the key leaders from our conference was on the scene and he decided he was going to stick with her while she went to get the car. This was a good thing as she was in a bit of a panic state, and when they got into the parking structure, she was disoriented and had no idea where the jeep was parked. As they ran up a couple rows of cars, she decided to hit the panic button on the key fob to get the horn going. Thankfully she was close enough to the vehicle when she did this and they quickly covered the two more rows of cars to find the jeep blaring away in our parking spot. They sped to the hotel entrance and the EMS team assisted me into the jeep. This was not exactly the way I would have ever envisioned my first 'run' to be like, but I guess we all need to start somewhere. It is just my way to make it a memorable one I guess. Luckily, we had calmed down while we were waiting in the ER for the doctors to finish my assessment. I was quite the sight with most of my head wrapped with white bandages and gauze sticking out of my mouth. I am not sure why Shelly found it so funny, but once she started laughing at my appearance, we were both laughing and struggled to gain composure. I guess it was a moment of stress release for us both. Thankfully I did not have any serious damage and our dentist and oral surgeon back at home were able to replace my broken tooth. That day was not only surreal but also seemed like a blur. That experience slowed my enthusiasm to begin my own running journey, but it was not bad enough to fully close the door on that dream. It just delayed my willingness to try for a few more years.

For years, I continued to accompany Shelly to races and played an active role with her as co-ambassadors for Ainsley's Angels in South Carolina. I am continuously inspired by our angel-athletes and could feel an internal desire inside myself to someday be an angel-runner. *But what about my nerve and muscle damage and what about my seizures? How would I ever be able to run, let alone push one of our angel-riders in a racing chariot?* These questions would often enter my mind, but something internally was telling me, despite these concerns, I needed to define what my abilities were, turn them into strengths and go from there. Fast forward to February of 2018, when Shelly decided to sign up for a two-day, four-race challenge in Tampa, Florida. This was a challenge event and included a 15K and a 5K on Saturday and a half-marathon and 8K on Sunday. She would be running with our good friends, who are all established endurance runners. They are a great group of people who make you better by just being around them. I would be going on the trip as well and my job was not only to be the best spectator and cheer squad for them all but also to be the team photographer. We were excited for the trip, and when the time came to make the journey, we all loaded into one big vehicle to make the trek. It was on this trip, at the race expo, that the seeds already planted for my own running journey would take root.

The Gasparilla Race Expo was one of the largest race expos we have been to. The Tampa Convention Center was loaded with vendors who had anything and everything to do with running. Walking into that venue made us feel like we were big kids in a candy store. There was so much action, energy and many interesting booths we wanted to check out. The one downfall was there was so much walking involved. Not only did we walk to the Convention Center from where we were staying but there was also a lot of square footage to cover once inside. I would be lying if I said that the walking was not fatiguing and hard on my legs. But Shelly was excited and wanted to check out many of the booths. I was ready to head back to the house to rest before getting ready for dinner when Shelly noticed something interesting. She spotted a booth where Bart Yasso, Runner's World's Chief Running Officer, was doing book signings. As Shelly got into the back of the line to wait our turn and speak to him, I went to sit down for a bit. As she waited, she noticed a woman behind the table on the opposite side of his booth. In front of this woman was a stack of books. As she got closer and could better see the cover of the book, Shelly noticed it had a cyclist on the front cover. *That's odd,* she thought to herself. *Why would a book by Bart have a cyclist on the front cover?* Then she noticed the title: *Gratitude in Motion.* "Michael!" she called out to me. "Come and check this out!" I was exhausted and not in the mood to stand in line. I was ready to leave. But Shelly persisted, and as I approached her, she moved out of her place in Bart's line and shifted over to the other side of the booth and in front of this woman. Not only had the title of the book caught Shelly's attention but the fact that it had a cyclist on the cover also really resonated with us both. The woman at the booth was Colleen Kelly Alexander, the author of that book. As we started talking to her and asking her about the book, she began to share her story. It was incredible to listen to her share about her life and a traumatic cycling accident she had survived. She had been run over by a freight truck while out training on her bike for an upcoming triathlon. She had nearly been killed and it was a true miracle she was still alive. We were captivated by her story, her life and her transformation post-accident. This was a pivotal moment for so many reasons. Colleen was easy to talk to and she was willing to share so openly about the amount of trauma she had endured and the struggles she continued to have in her recovery. As she talked, I was taken aback by her smile and her ability to show much gratitude for her life and the blessings she had along her journey. *Gratitude in Motion* was definitely the right title for her book! And to make it even more impressive, she shared how she was working hard to get back to running and cycling despite having catastrophic injuries. As we talked, I shared a little of my own story. The conference center was crazy busy, but for us, it felt as if the entire room had been silenced. Colleen gave us her full and undivided attention and was genuinely interested in my story and our own journey. As I looked at her, I felt my confidence rising. I told Colleen, "Someday, I'm going to run." She looked me straight in the eyes and said, "If you do, I will run with you." Of course I told her I would be honored to have her run with me, but I really did not believe she actually meant what she said. We continued talking and both Shelly and I bought a book and had her autograph it for us. As we walked away and back through the expo to meet up with our friends, we stopped and Shelly said, "You know she was serious, don't you? If you decide to do a race, I believe she will show up and run with you. You will have to keep in touch with her." Still stunned, I had a hard time believing this. But she had inspired and motivated me. Like me, Colleen was someone who had been through something so traumatic and debilitating, it had changed her life physically, mentally and emotionally. Yet, in only a few years, she had worked hard through her recovery and was now racing again. She was the first person I had personally met who could relate to and understand what it was I had been through and how hard it was to get out there and run. Through the rest of that night and weekend, I could not stop thinking about Colleen and her story. Her strength, grit and determination had captivated me. Could she have been serious? Would she really run with me? Shelly was confident she had been serious, and I felt that hungry feeling in my gut that running could truly become a reality for me. That chance encounter at a busy race expo in a state hundreds of miles away had ignited the flame of belief in my soul. I now believed I would one day run again.

Once we had returned home, I could not stop thinking about meeting Colleen. It was one of those moments in your life that you know you were in the right place, at the right time, for the right reason. I was still a bit shy about reaching out to her, but Shelly kept encouraging me to do so. What did I have to lose? All she could do was say 'no.' So I did what most people do today in our digital world. I connected with her on Facebook and sent her a direct message. My intent was to thank her for our conversation at the expo and let her know we loved her book. After that initial connection, she sent me a message back and asked if I could share with her more about my story. I quickly sent her a link to a website I had created. I had created this website not only to share our story but also to continue rehab on my hands and fingers after my accident. I still did not fully believe she would run with me, but I was grateful for the fire she had lit within me. Within an hour, Colleen reached back out to me and asked me more questions. Her questions started with "You were actually paralyzed? Hit cows?" Then the key question came through: "When are we going to run?"

Holy Cow! It was official. Colleen and her husband, Sean, wanted to come to South Carolina and run a race with us. But there was one big problem. I had to learn how to run. I guess the first step was to buy some running shoes and then go from there. So off we went to our favorite local running store, Fleet Feet Myrtle Beach, to buy a good pair of shoes. With a powerful vision and focus, I had taken a couple of major first steps. Now it was time to hit the pavement. My running journey had begun.

I must admit I was a little nervous on that first day. I laced up my shoes and headed out the door. From my driveway and mailbox, I set off and ran to the next-door neighbor's mailbox. Yep, I did it. It may not have been a long distance, but I accomplished my goal. I did not fall. I ran back to my house and then did a repeat of this, going a bit farther to the end of our cul-de-sac and back. With my heart pounding and a strong sense of accomplishment, I thought to myself, *I am a runner!* Day two would take me a little farther and then some. More the day after that, and I quickly discovered that I really could run. It was not pretty, and I certainly was not going to break any records anytime soon, but I was running. It was my pace, my race, my way. It was apparent from the onset that shoes were going to be more important than I realized. Because my right leg fatigues quickly, I actually drag and scuff my right foot along the pavement every time I step with it. This is not a good thing for the health or longevity of your running shoes. I found myself tearing up my shoes after a few short runs. Shelly said I really needed to concentrate on my form and strength on my right side. With sore, bruised toes and ripped-up shoes we went back to the running store. This time we had a new awareness of what my running form would be and how critical it was for me to have the right shoes for my unique running stride. Our friend Chelsea was working that day and knew exactly what I needed for long-term success. She introduced me to the shoes which would become the only ones for me. They were from a company called Altra and they had a wide toe box and balanced cushion-ing important for so many people but critical for me. They felt great on my feet, as my toes had room to naturally spread out. I felt almost as if I was rolling through my steps. I was excited to get back out on the road.

I felt like things were falling into place. I ran a little farther every day, still at my pace and my way, but with confidence growing along with my strength. I had not yet tripped or fallen, and I had not yet had a seizure while running. So far, so good! It was surreal because more than ever, I slowly felt like I was now part of a bigger team. Moving from the sidelines toward the finish line of my dreams, I was determined to demolish once again that prediction that I would never walk again. I was going to show those doctors and anyone who had doubted me what I was made of and capable of doing. I was surrounded by great friends, amazing athletes and of course my biggest cheerleader and love of my life who helped to encourage me and lift me up through my efforts. I was a student of positivity and surrounded by the strength of an incredible human spirit. In addition to my own training, Shelly thought it would be beneficial to hire a running coach. We knew the perfect person who had the knowledge, patience and willingness to take on a challenging client like me. I may have proved to be the toughest assignment he ever had, but coach Frank was the perfect person. Frank Pepp is a fast, experienced, knowledgeable runner and coach. He is a barefoot runner and an eight-time qualifier in the Boston Marathon and has run it seven times. On top of his lengthy resume, Frank is very intelligent and curious. A continuous student of many topics, Frank knew I was not going to shatter any records. He did not hesitate to accept the challenge of working with and training me, and I believe he was excited to have been asked to support my journey. He immediately started asking me more questions about my spinal cord injury and seizures and got to work on making deeper assessments of my running style, current level of strength and abilities. He also got to work researching and studying any/all information he could find relating to my scenario. After he learned more about me and my situation, he created a plan and structure, which together would strengthen me into the athlete that I am today. I had the heart, vision and determination to run a race. Frank had the tactics on how to make that happen. He was the person who would take my dream and literally walk/ run with me to its fruition.

As training progressed and the stress of running with Colleen and Sean mounted, Shelly and I created a plan to make my first run in over 20 years a special one. We had always believed that if you were blessed, you needed to BECOME a blessing to others. Sitting on the sidelines and dreaming of someday running a race myself, part of that dream included running with Ainsley's Angels and pushing an angel-rider in a race. My first race would be a 5K, running with Ainsley's Angels. And I knew exactly who I wanted that angel-rider to be. Her name is Faith. She is beautiful, bright, has an incredible spirit and smile, and she was exactly whom I needed to be with me and inspire me to the finish line. And Faith LOVES to race! 'Faith to the Finish Line' had a beautiful ring and meaning for me. But if you knew Faith and her amazing mom, Wonder Woman Candace, you would understand how special this moment was going to be. Faith is not only her name—it is who she is. She can bring out the best in anyone, and she and her mom have a strong faith and belief in Christ. After presenting the idea to Candace and Faith, we were grateful they accepted. It became official. Together, we were going to take our Faith to the finish line.

Shelly and I thought the Myrtle Beach Mini Marathon weekend would be the perfect time to plan my race. That weekend included the Coastal 5K, perfect for my plan! It is a popular race during the fall and has a strong attendance. As we communicated details to Colleen and Sean, Shelly and I thought it would be a good idea to include our local partners in the plans. I thought if I was going to do my first 5K, why not create a 'Dream Team' to share the excitement with. The idea was captivating, and we slowly put the idea into motion. Each person we approached was excited for me and eagerly said yes when asked if they would be part of my special day. Our friends at Fleet Feet Myrtle Beach opened their hearts and doors to us and allowed us to host a night at their store. Colleen and Sean would travel from Massachusetts and do a speaking engagement and book signing at the Fleet Feet store. A very good friend secured an oceanfront room at the Myrtle Beach Marriott for them to stay. We then gathered a group of friends to inspire me to the finish line. The group included Shelly, Coach Frank, Colleen and Sean and our good friends Terry and Johnna Terragna. It also included Paul Rogers, the owner of Fleet Feet, a couple of local running friends and some special friends who travelled in from Columbia, South Carolina. These friends run for RWB, a running group that supports veterans. My simple mission to someday run a 5K with Shelly was turning into a full-scale event.

As the race weekend approached, the excitement grew. It was going to be special in so many ways. One critical unknown remained. Could I go the distance and successfully push Faith to the finish line? I was nervous but I was getting stronger by the day. Unbeknownst to me, Shelly had a few little surprises up her sleeve, and she did a great job keeping them secret. First, Dream Team shirts were being created by Terry and Paul for our little team. And Shelly was working behind the scenes to have some special guests at the race. We woke up early on race morning and arrived at our strategically placed Ainsley's Angels trailer. Team Faith was not the only AAA team participating in this race. We had multiple teams of angels who would be doing this alongside us. As I walked up to the trailer, the door was already open and racing chariots were being prepared by good friends who had taken over for us. Ainsley's Angels truly is a family, and we had our very own precious one, the Ross family, handling all the logistical details of the day. Adam, Elizabeth and their four children are such a blessing to us and our community. My nerves had my stomach fluttering, and I was anxious and excited at the same time as I approached the group who was already there. Out of the shadows I saw a few people walking out of the trailer and toward us. As I peered at them through the darkness of the morning, I did a double take. I couldn't believe it. Was that my family? I looked at Shelly in confusion as my mind tried to take in what I was seeing. Walking toward me were my sisters, Mary and Kathleen, and Kathy's daughter, Jordan, and son, Cameron. I was shocked and then overtaken by emotion. I could not comprehend how they were there. Hugs, tears and laughter started to flow as we all embraced and cried together. I could not believe Shelly pulled this off without me, the investigator, not having a clue. They had flown in the night before, just in time to make it to the race. And the final surprise? Cameron was going to run with one of our angel teams. A first time for him. We were so excited and pumped up! Now the pressure was on. It was time to get the party started.

As the people from the rest of our teams arrived at the trailer I was overwhelmed with gratitude. I was surrounded by friends and family who were there to support me and to support our angel teams. Not only did my family surprise me but so many other precious friends also came out that morning to cheer me on. Good friends Rose and Don, Patricia and Brent and Mona had all also shown up to surprise me and cheer me on.

Many running friends were out with signs to cheer me on and support our teams. Love and joy surrounded us all. I still could not believe Colleen and Sean made the trip to run with us. The Dream Team was a power group of incredible people, and they were ready to go, especially Faith. You could feel the energy in the air as all our angels and their families arrived. We had six Angel teams total in the race, and each one of our riders and runners was pumped and ready to roll. After Faith was carefully loaded into her beautiful pink racing chariot. I proudly stood behind it as we all started to move toward the start. The moment was a bit surreal. As we walked along with other runners in the waning darkness of the morning, I could hear the announcer and I saw the crowd for the first time as a runner. What a moment! With my nervous system attempting to take over the right side of my body, I quickly realized I was going to have to concentrate on every step to go the distance.

As we walked, Shelly had been walking ahead with a group of people. Suddenly she had people calling out to her. She turned around and looked in our direction and immediately realized I was having a seizure. She sprinted back to me and stayed with me as the seizure worked through my body. Friends who were near realized what was happening and they all stayed close to ensure I was ok. This was not exactly the way I would have scripted my first run, but having a seizure, while not fun or fair, is a part of who I am and one of the many life's obstacles I must maneuver. It just heightened the significance of that day for those around us. It provided a greater depth of understanding of what I deal with too often. After I had fully come out of the seizure state, we continued as a group, united together even more as we fell into line at the front of the field of runners to start the race. The encouragement, cheering crowd and signs of encouragement were unbelievable. After a quick announcement about Ainsley's Angels, the gun went off and we were off. Our angel teams were in the front of the field of runners and started off the race. It was an incredible feeling to be running, pushing Faith and to be surrounded by my own team of angels. My Dream Team. It is hard to explain in words the feelings and power being on that race route had for me. I have heard others try to describe this feeling before, but nothing had prepared me for the intensity of the moment and emotion. As we raced along, Shelly was her usual cheerleader self, shouting out words of encouragement not only for Faith and me and our team but also for others who were passing us. She ran ahead to take pictures of our group, high-fiving others as they passed her. The smiles in the pictures tell the story more than any words can ever say. As we neared the final turn to the finish line, someone called out, "I can see the finish line!" I looked at Shelly and said, "Are we actually there? I can't see the finish line! Where is it?!" She calmly responded telling me it was just around the corner. She helped to calm my nerves as she talked through the strategy of being careful as we entered the finish area. There was a quick turn into a downhill entry to the finish line. The route also started to become narrower at this point and I would have to concentrate fully to keep not only myself and Faith safe but also other runners coming in. I held onto that chair with all the strength I had, as I felt my legs starting to lock up with the adrenaline and excitement of this moment. Not only did my Dream Team still surround me but Cameron also rejoined us after he had finished his own race, as did a couple of other friends. Our friend Mya, from RWB, had been running steadily along right behind me, carrying the American flag the entire time. What a sight we were that day! It may sound selfish but all I could think of that day was Faith and our own team. It was so magical.

It felt like it had taken forever, but we finally crossed that finish line. Holy Cow! I was officially a runner! That is, I had just finished my first running race ever and had earned my first medal. More importantly, we had taken Faith to the Finish Line. With Faith, how could someone ever have had fear? With her leading the way, it was a mission accomplished!

TWENTY

IT'S NOT OVER YET

I have told you all this so that you may have peace in me.
Here on earth you will have many trials and sorrows. But
take heart, because I have overcome the world.

—*John 16:33*

So... where do we go from here? One thing is for sure, it is not over yet! We have lived a lot of life in our 55+ years (as of the writing of this book) on this planet. Michael and I both feel we have barely just begun. We feel we are on the cusp of something great which we were meant to do with our lives. We have so much passion, energy and desire to take the learnings from our life lessons and share them with others. We have gone through challenging and/or troubling times and we have struggled to make it through. We have figured out so much of it ourselves along the way and have made more than our fair share of mistakes doing it. So often, we have thought to ourselves, *If only we had had someone to share with us then what we know now. Life could have been so much easier if we would have had some help through many different experiences from others who had travelled down a similar path.* We understand the value of insight from others who have already travelled certain roads similar to ours and the lessons which can be learned from them. Today, technology allows the sharing of information and stories and opens an entirely new world of help, support and resources. We firmly believe we did not go through all the struggles we have gone through and to have received all the wonderful gifts and blessings we have received just to keep those for ourselves. No, God has blessed us so that we can take those blessings and what we have learned to help others in some way. Our struggles must count for something! We are here to do a greater good. Each of us only gets one chance at this life, and it is not meant for us to live in our own individual small, little box. We are all equipped with our own unique sets of skills, abilities, characteristics and strengths. Our pastor at church delivers fabulous messages which speak right to our hearts and souls. Pastor Clay NeSmith, from Barefoot Church in North Myrtle Beach, South Carolina, has a great gift of being able to send a message to a large room filled with people. Afterward, the common theme heard amongst those in attendance is "I felt as if he were speaking directly to me." He has a true gift from God—not only to connect with his audience but also to leave each person with a 'Call to Action' message. As you have already read, one of our favorite mantras is 'Use what you have, do what you can.' This came from Pastor Clay. One such weekend, as we listened to him with intensity and emotion, we heard him say, "We all, each of us, need to use what we have and do what we can." Yes!!! This spoke directly to both Michael and I and our belief system in why we are here on this earth. It has inspired us in so many ways and we often catch ourselves using this phrase in projects we are working on. Use what we have. Do what we can. Anyone and everyone has an opportunity to give in some way to this world with that concept.

The magic is in the mess. When I realize it is not a game of perfection, this allows me to look at things differently. I can pick my head up, look around and see what is truly around me. What am I doing? What am I missing? People are drawn to you when you are more vulnerable and authentic. The 'fake persona' is not attractive to most people for long. I think of Michael when he has his seizures. Every single time he has one, I feel closer to him and love him more than ever. Every time. The funny thing is, he has tried to hide them his entire life. He was embarrassed by them and felt like others would look at him differently if they knew what was really going on with him. He still thinks that way even though he has been working very hard to shift that paradigm of thought. What he needs to fully understand is that most people do think a bit differently of him once they witness him struggle through a seizure. Most love him more and respect him more, as it showcases the struggles he has on a continual basis. Despite that struggle, look at what he is doing with his life. What many do not understand is it is not despite that struggle; it is because of it. The magic is in the mess. When people understand the depth of what he deals with, it makes that which he can accomplish and his attitude toward life and others that much more powerful. His power comes from being his true authentic self. That is where your superpower comes from as well. When you let the light and energy of your true authentic self shine through, the possibilities of what you can accomplish are limitless. The question is, what barriers are you going to put up around yourself which will limit all you have to share with the world? Maybe it's time to move those barriers away for good. What do you have which you can use to help others? Who can benefit from what you have learned from your own experiences? Use what you have, do what you can.

Keep moving. Moving your body as much as you can, as often as you can is key to your longevity and quality of life not only now but also for your future. You know that old adage 'use it or lose it'? Well, there is much truth to that. We have lived it ourselves and have witnessed the negative effects in others from not staying active. Obviously, Michael's story of being paralyzed and the significant impact his mindset and rehabilitation had on his ability to regain mobility is a powerful one. He worked extremely hard through the entire process and continuously pushed himself each day, often beyond what the doctors or therapists were asking for or even expecting of him. He continues to do that to this day. He was the only one who could do the work. Others were not able to do it for him. If he had stayed in a negative place mentally or had resisted the exercises and tasks because they were uncomfortable for him or caused him pain, he could possibly still be in a wheelchair today. We witnessed the physical toll it took on my mom when she moved from her townhouse, which was three stories, to a one-story cottage home. In the townhouse, she was forced to utilize all three stories of her home each day due to the design of it. As much as we worried about the stairs being a hazard for her as she was aging, they were very beneficial for her to use those muscles in her legs she was not challenged to use once she moved. The effects of not using those muscles showed up quickly after she moved. Her legs became very weak, and she began to be very unstable in her footing. Most of her life she had always been on her feet, very busy and active in her job and at home, rarely sitting down to rest. She became much more sedentary after she moved to the cottage, and it soon became a struggle for her to walk any distance. Little by little, everyday actions such as moving from a seated position to a standing one or vice versa became not only a challenge but also a safety hazard. We watched her become more fearful and unsteady in her own movements. This was very difficult and sad to witness, and we urged her to join a gym to challenge those muscles she was not moving. We even bought her a series of personal trainer sessions so she had an expert who could help her rebuild some strength and stability. This was something she was not experienced with and definitely not comfortable with, and these ideas never really took hold for her. She tried by getting out to walk when the weather was good, but she just never regained that everyday routine of challenging different muscles. It did not take long at all for her to lose that muscle tone and strength and stability in moving her body. The older we get, the harder it is and the longer it will take to recover. So do not stop moving and challenging yourself every single day. Staying active means different things to different people. It could mean exercising and being involved in sports such as running, biking, swimming, skiing, playing hockey, whatever. It could also mean dancing, walking with your dog or friends and neighbors, picking up shells along the beach, walking the course when you play golf instead of riding in the cart, etc. Do something radical like volunteer with a group to 'Adopt-a-Highway' and help to clean up your community by picking up trash. Not only will you be moving and exercising, using many different muscles, but you will also meet new people and clean up portions of the ridiculous amount of trash we see out in our environments every day. It could mean something as simple as parking in the back of the parking lot so you have longer to walk to get to your store or destination, taking the stairs instead of the elevator or getting up to walk around your house, office or building every hour or so. It could mean playing in the park or yard with your kids, vacuuming the house and going up/down the stairs to do your laundry. Whatever you can do to move your body and challenge as many muscles as you can, do it and do it regularly. You are looking for that 1% slight edge effect, to do 1% more today than you did yesterday. Do not worry about someone else's results—they are not yours. You need to focus on your own progress and strive to push yourself a bit more each day.

We feel very strongly that food is medicine. We could write a whole new book on this subject. What we eat has a distinct and profound impact on the health of our bodies. You are either feeding disease or fighting it with each bite you take. The negative impacts from a poor diet may not be felt for a long time, maybe even decades, but they will be felt one way or the other. The beautiful thing is we have the power to change that outcome right now. Every time you put something in your mouth, whatever it is you consume, it will have an impact on the health of your body. This can have a good impact or not. This philosophy ties in as a great example of what we mentioned above, about wishing we knew then what we know now. We have many years of poor eating habits and lifestyle choices we wish we could go back, erase and do over. But we can't. What if back in our 20s or 30s, or even earlier, we had had someone share with us the extensive amount of scientific evidence having a whole-plant diet would have on our long-term health? Maybe we could have prevented some health challenges we have had to deal with. But now, we can only work hard today to make the right choices going forward. After years of being involved in sports and researching different tactics we could use to make ourselves feel better, be stronger and be more successful at what we were working to accomplish, we have learned a lot! We have been working on cleaning up our nutritional habits for years and we now live a whole-plant nutritional lifestyle. That's right, we eat plants. We do not eat any items which come from any animal. We eat what is grown, not what is born. There is a tremendous amount of information and numerous scientific studies which showcase the incredible healthy benefits having a plant-based diet has on the body. It can have the power to not only keep many diseases at bay, but it has been shown to reverse many conditions and diseases which are common in our western culture. We have seen this have a profound impact on our own health and well-being, particularly with me. In 2019, I was diagnosed with an ovarian mass and had surgery to remove the 17-pound mass. Yes! You read that correctly. It was 17 pounds! I lost 35 pounds of weight the week of my surgery due to not only the mass but also all the fluids built up from inflammation and infection. That was a very scary time for us both, especially for me. The surgery was a great success, and we thought the surgery would be the worst of it. We believed once that was complete, I would be on the road to recovery and full healing. We later found out my health was still in jeopardy and further treatment was advised beyond the surgery. We did an extensive amount of research and connected with different doctors around the country, as well as had a great support system offering heavy prayer for my healing. In the end, I decided to take a holistic approach to my ongoing 'treatment' and continuing 'medicine.' I chose to utilize diet and lifestyle choices for treatment. We went 100% into the whole-plant diet world and immersed ourselves in as much study and information as we possibly could. We spent hours, days, weeks and months reading, listening and researching information. In fact, this has not stopped yet. We do continuous education through involvement in health summits, podcasts, reading books written by various doctors, watching documentaries on the subject matter and more. We attended Plant-Stock in the fall of 2019. Plant-Stock is an entire weekend packed with speakers, professionals and doctors teaching and sharing modules on how food affects the body. That fall, upon returning from Plant-Stock, I took an online three-month plant-based cooking class. I did this so that we could have the tools and knowledge to put this lifestyle into action. We have never eaten so much incredible and flavorful food as we have in the past few years. It has been AMAZING!!! We feel stronger, healthier and more powerful than we have ever felt in our lives. What we have learned along the way is to not be a victim to your circumstances but become a victor for yourself by choosing what is the right path for you and those you love. This choice is different for us all. But we will continue to share with others the power and wonder a whole-plant diet can have on a higher quality of life and hopefully improve longevity. This also happens to be a way of life and eating which falls into other very critical views we have on animal welfare and the impacts on the health of our planet. We have the power to make a difference in every action we take, including what we choose to put in our mouths. We will not know the full impact this lifestyle choice will have for us until our final days, but we do know now what an improved level of health and well-being it has had on us thus far.

Own your vulnerability and stand tall in what you are achieving because of it. When you think about your own story, think of the most difficult, negative and challenging experiences you have been through. As dark as those moments and days were, what positive change has been brought into your life because of those experiences? What people were brought into your life you may never have met had you not gone through that experience? What did you learn about yourself now that you look back at how you handled those situations? What skills or abilities were discovered or created because of the challenges you had to overcome? When Michael made that most difficult decision to step away from his career, doing a job he loved to do, because of epilepsy and a seizure disorder, he was scared. That was his identity. What he did for a living was his life. It was where he spent most of his time and energy, creating his persona. Who was he without catching shoplifters and handling theft and fraud? Who would he be without being a part of a larger team and company doing amazing things in communities all over this nation? He struggled with this for a while. It did not help matters that this all happened at the same time we moved to a new area where we did not yet know anyone. We moved to a neighborhood outside of the city. One you must drive to get to. And he was no longer driving. Meanwhile, I was working many hours, 45 minutes away, as I transitioned into my new store and role with the company. Michael was essentially trapped at home. Saying it was a challenging time is an understatement. But he knew he needed to do something different. It was time for him to recreate himself. What did he want to do with his life? Who was he going to be in this new world of his? That dark time of his life helped him to create and discover new skills and interests he would have previously never realized he had. He always had a strong passion to help others. He taught himself how to build a website to share our story. His 'why' for doing this was multi-purposeful. It was a task to continue to stretch and strengthen the dexterity of his hands and fingers. It was also meant to stretch his mindset and level of knowledge. And it was a desire to share hope and inspiration with a mission to help someone else going through difficult times. He discovered a passion for photography. He now had time to slow down and view the world with a new vision. All those years waiting and watching for signs of theft, fraud and wrongdoing honed an ability in him to see the world through a different lens. He has a natural gift to capture some of this essence on camera. He realized he could take this skill and be creative with it by making videos, memory books, social media posts and more. Having the ability to spend his time in life differently than being at work all the time, he discovered new-found passions in cycling, running, creating and volunteering with nonprofit organizations, strengthening his faith and relationship with God, adopting and caring for fur babies, traveling and more. It has been a life lesson of rearranging priorities for us both. Unfortunately, for many, it often takes going through something difficult to slow down, look around and realize what and who is most important in our lives. Maybe by reading our story, it might help someone else realize that for themselves before they miss out or go through a really dark place to get there.

Using your passion for purpose. Isn't this an incredible life goal for us all? We hear this often, to do what you love and create your life around it. But who really gets to do that? For so many of us, life gets in the way. We start out by choosing a path which we think we desire, only to find out down the road, after much time, energy and money invested into it, that it really is not what truly drives us in life. Sometimes we think it is too late for us to change. That ship has sailed, and we missed the boat. We are here to tell you this is not the case! It is never too late to do what you love. It may take creative planning, more time than you care to give, applying yourself differently in order to accomplish your goals, but it is still possible. Do not let life pass you by, thinking *I wish*, or *I could have but I didn't*. This may not mean shifting careers. It could mean something as simple and as easy as taking up a new hobby, trying a new activity or becoming involved with a program or charity which touches your heart. One thing we have discovered for ourselves is that we are nowhere near fulfilled unless we are working to help others. Living this life is so much more than just about you. It is about sharing the best of you with others. God created you for a very important reason. That is to share your gifts and talents with the world. He created a masterpiece in you, and He does not make mistakes. The gifts you have and the lessons you have learned, someone else needs those too. Use what you have, do what you can. So… our question to you is: What are you going to do with your story?

ACKNOWLEDGEMENTS

Over the years, as we have shared our story, a common response has emerged. "Holy Cow!" is the first natural response by many people, followed by "You two need to write a book." The vision and dream of ours to share our story in the hopes of helping others had been simmering in our pot of thoughts for years. Not having children of our own, it also provided us a tool to leave some type of legacy in this world to live beyond our own lives. The experience of writing this book has allowed us to revel in the memories of the many people who have been significant to us along the way.

We have been blessed with many amazing people in our lives. Some so deep and intertwined with our roots they are part of our core and DNA. Others have passed through our lives like a season, adding and nourishing for growth at that time and then moving along like leaves blowing in the wind. The most significant people in our lives are our family. They are the ones we struggle most to find the words to adequately share our love and gratitude. Because of your unconditional love, support and encouragement, you have given us the strength and courage to stand and walk toward our dreams. Regardless of the geographical distance between us, our bond and love for you has only grown stronger as the years have passed.

To our Target family, how can we thank you all enough? If not for our career choice with Target, Shelly and I may have never met. If not for the opportunities provided during our tenure, who knows where we would be today? Our lives would be so different, and we would not have met the many wonderful people who have crossed our paths as we travelled along on our journey to the coast of the Carolinas. We are forever grateful to all of you who shared your love and support during our darkest days and who were there to lift us up and offer an open road for us to continue our journey together. Oh, the memories we have from so many years together. Those memories continue to fill us with fondness, laughter and stories to tell. Great people attract great people, and we were fortunate to be surrounded by so many in our Target family. We are blessed for those lifelong friendships, memories and the growth and development from the opportunities we had.

To the medical professionals who are responsible for the phenomenal care and service you provided during so many challenging moments in our lives, Thank You! Without your level of skill, expertise and compassion, our lives would be drastically different today. You have been part of our team and have literally allowed me the ability to rise and walk. How do you say "Thank You" to those who help to give a person their mobility back? Those who enhance the level of hope and desire to help keep dreams alive? You are changing lives every day, not just for the patients you serve, but also for the caregivers who love and surround those patients. Bless you all!

To our many friends, who we could not possibly list you all here, but who have had a profound impact in our lives, we love you and are so grateful for every one of you. You are our family away from family. You fill our days with love, joy, laughter, support and fun, and we cherish our moments together. So many memories we have created with you and so many more are in our future together. God has surrounded us with the most wondrous people, and we are honored and blessed to have each of you in our lives.

To our Ainsley's Angels Family, Thank You! You have added such a level of depth, significance and purpose to our lives which we could never have imagined for ourselves. From that first phone call with Michelle Kendall Smith, to the next phone call only hours later with Kim Rooster Rossiter, we knew immediately we were 'home'. How can an organization of volunteers grow from humble beginnings of only two ambassadorship locations, to over 30,000 strong in 34 states, 70 locations and still be growing? It is a testament to the power of 'family' and the level of love shown by all who are part of our AAA family. This would not be possible without the impact one little girl made in her short life in this world and the willingness her precious family had to share her and their journey with us all. Their drive, commitment and passion to share her story and to create her legacy is a profound gift touching more lives than any of us will ever imagine. We are honored and proud to be a part of this extraordinary organization.

For all those people who told us 'we couldn't'? Thank You! You instilled in us a drive deeper than we could have ever imagined. This drive has helped us to showcase not only that we could, but we would, and we did. We feel we are only just getting started. Stay tuned. There is so much more to come.

ABOUT THE AUTHORS

Michael and Shelly Warner are a plant-powered husband and wife team who are passionate that living a healthy lifestyle is the elixir to living a life of significance. They have realized the fragility of life and how precious it is through the adversity they have endured together. Branding themselves as 'Team Warner', they have designed a lifestyle in which they can demonstrate the power of shared values. Thriving despite injury and illness, and utilizing their skills developed after a combined forty-five years of operational and security retail leadership, their mission is to help others believe in the impossible. Having an emphasis on the exceptional needs community, their mission is to lead by being active, healthy and sharing lessons learned along the way. With thousands of miles run and cycled, including five full marathons, numerous half marathons, three centurion bike rides and countless other finish line experiences, Team Warner has illustrated that no obstacle is too large. Fueled by plants and driven by purpose, they utilize gratitude to power their passions. They believe when blessed, you should be a blessing to others. This belief has inspired them to utilize the world of adaptive sports to make a greater impact. Not only were they original founders of South Carolina's first Paralympic Sports Club, they were later emboldened to bring Ainsley's Angels of America to South Carolina. With a passion for running and cycling, this was the perfect fit to serve through endurance events. Believing anyone can achieve their goals, they hope to motivate you and inspire you to live your best self. God created each of us for significance, and they hope their shared experiences and passions encourage you to take the next step on your own journey. Don't miss the moments!

Michael and Shelly are originally from Michigan and currently reside in South Carolina with their dog, Nevo and two cats, Pinot and Espy.